C000095165

managing
CORPORATE
reputations

managing
CORPORATE
reputations

edited by ADAM JOLLY

PRca
PUBLIC
RELATIONS
consultants
association

KOGAN
PAGE

First published in 2001

Kogan Page Limited
120 Pentonville Road
London N1 9JN

© Kogan Page and contributors, 2001

British Library Cataloguing in Publication Data

ISBN 0 7494 3488 0

Typeset by Saxon Graphics Ltd, Derby
Printed and bound in Great Britain by Biddles Ltd
www.biddles.co.uk

Contents

Foreword   vii
Dr Tom Watson, Chairman of the Public Relations
Consultants Assocation

PART 1: Impacts   **1**
1.1   Why reputation matters   3
      Ketchum, a unit of the Omnicom Group Inc.
1.2   What makes a good corporate reputation   7
      Adrian Wheeler, CEO of GCI UK
1.3   Managing reputation in the internet age   12
      Andrew Laurence, Joint Chief Executive of
      Hill & Knowlton UK, and Matthew Blakstad,
      Head of Interactive Practice
1.4   Reputation's return on investment   20
      Jack Bergen, President of the Council of Public
      Relations Firms
1.5   Measuring reputation   27
      Chris Genasi, Chief Executive Corporate of
      Weber Shandwick Worldwide

PART 2: Expectations   **35**
2.1   Global campaigns & communications   37
      Graham Lancaster, Chairman of Biss Lancaster Euro RSCG
2.2   Consumers' contradictory expectations   42
      Ira Matathia, CEO, and Marian Salzman,
      Worldwide Director, The Intelligence Factory
2.3   Managing the pressure   47
      Sara Render, Chief Executive of Kinross & Render
2.4   Communities & gains   54
      Dr Tom Watson, Chairman of the Public Relations
      Consultants Association, and Steve Osborne-Brown,
      Account Director of Hallmark Public Relations
2.5   Public policy and regulators   60
      Simon Nayyar, Executive Director of Citigate Public Affairs
2.6   Investor relations   64
      Brian Basham, Equity.i.Group

2.7   Organisational culture and change   68
      Colette Dorward, Partner, Smythe Dorward Lambert
2.8   Employee expectations   72
      Tari Hibbitt, Chief Executive of Edelman

PART 3: Responses   **79**
3.1   Unified communications structures   81
      John Williams, Fishburn Hedges
3.2   Recruiting & rewarding professionals   87
      Harris Diamond, President and Chief Executive of
      BSMG Worldwide
3.3   Managing corporate reputation through crisis   91
      Michael Regester, Founding Partner of Regester Larkin
3.4   Launching products & services   104
      Lesley Brend, Managing Director of The RED Consultancy
3.5   Reputations online   108
      Mark Mellor, Director of Firefly
3.6   Managing market sentiment   114
      Tim Kitchin, Ogilvy PR
3.7   Evaluating messages   118
      Sandra Macleod, Chief Executive of Echo Research
3.8   The logistics of name changes   122
      Claire Meredith, Sodexho Alliance

PART 4: Directory of PRCA Members   **129**
The Public Relations Consultancy Association   131

PART 5: Directory of ICCO Members   **175**
The International Communications Consultancy Organisation   177

PART 6: Appendix   **189**
List of Contributors   191

Foreword

Dr Tom Watson, Chairman of the Public Relations Consultants Association (PRCA)

'Never do anything you wouldn't want to be caught dead doing', was the advice from actor John Carradine to his son David, also an actor. It is a good rule of life that also applies to corporations, governments and individuals, yet so many ignore it.

This book is an important contribution to the discussion of corporate reputation and its management. The range of writers, their expertise and perspectives will add immensely to the knowledgeable understanding of public relations and enhance its own reputation as a valuable component of business strategy.

For too long, public relations has been seen as a delivery mechanism for selective messages. The strategic element of public relation practice has been conducted widely yet without fanfare. 'PR' has been seen as the province of spin doctors, Edinas and the gin & tonic brigade. I would like to wallow in the self-pity that the industry reputation is all the media's fault, like John Lydon who was notorious as the Sex Pistol's Johnny Rotten and tendentiously claimed in 1986 that 'my reputation is a media creation'.

However, that's not an option in a time when transparency is a demand and not a choice. Public relations is a strong and vital industry that is growing in all directions with increasing evidence of its value for business.

In the UK, the size – by fee earnings – of PRCA members has more than doubled in a decade. Worldwide, the PR industry is conservatively valued at £5 billion ($8 billion) a year in fee and related earnings. Growth is tracked at least 20 per cent a year and is often higher. In many countries, undergraduate training is widely offered and demand to enter the PR business continues to grow. PRCA's own evidence from its PReview new business enquiry service is of continuing growth in interest from quarter to quarter.

There's no doubt that businesses value public relations with as much vigour as Bill Gates of Microsoft who said, 'If I had one last marketing dollar, I would spend it on public relations'. Even though the IT industry has had a difficult time in 2000–2001, it has relied heavily on public relations in the massive expansion of previous years. Innovators like Microsoft and its competitors have adopted public relations practices to promote products, corporate positions and to build their reputations.

But in what directions will the PR industry move? Progress can be considered along a continuum from delivery only to strategy only. Twenty years ago, the PR industry was mostly concerned with delivery of messages, mainly via media relations. In recent times, greater emphasis has been put upon communications strategy that has been shaped by research and consultancy insights. I consider that the PR industry is half-way along that line between delivery and strategy and it will increasingly be concerned with planning and strategy as it moves to 25 per cent delivery and 75 per cent strategy.

As Jack Bergen, of the US's Council of PR Firms, notes in his article, *Reputation's Return on Investment*, that securities analysts consider that 30–50 per cent of the valuations placed on a company's shares are based on non-financial factors. That means the reputation of a company has a value to both develop and defend.

Strategic public relations combines both attributes. Unlike management consultants who primarily analyse issues and recommend change, the public relations practitioner, whether employed or a consultant, has to deliver the results of strategy. This is why public relations is so highly valued. Practitioners have their collective feet on the ground as well as being strong analysts of issues.

Within the gradual transition of public relations practice to the more strategic model, new techniques will be developed. Among them will be the cross-fertilisation of techniques from new media, negotiation, marketing metrics and closer alliances with business and communications academics.

New media has the highest profile, but other disciplines have many challenges and opportunities. Negotiation techniques, honed in international crises, can aid issues management and corporate social responsibility strategies; marketing metrics can influence the creation of PR metrics and be placed alongside financial indicators; link-ups with academics and business schools can place public relations into the main stream of discussions of Return on Investment (ROI) and business strategy.

But above all, the reputation and usage of public relations techniques will continue to rise at a rate that is at least similar to the second half of the 1990s and probably much faster.

Kogan Page is to be congratulated for proposing and publishing this book and my colleagues in the Public Relations Consultants Association and the International Communications Consultancy Organisation are commended for sponsoring it and, in many cases, writing its key chapters. The reputation of public relations lies with its practitioners and this book demonstrates that it is in good hands.

Dr Tom Watson is Chairman of the PRCA from 2000–2002. He is Managing Director of Hallmark Public Relations Ltd and gained his PhD in 1995 for research into evaluation of public relations programmes.

The Public Relations Consultants Association
Willow House
Willow Place
London
SW1P 1JH
T: 020 7233 6026
F: 020 7828 4797
E: info@prca.org.uk
W: www.prca.org.uk

1

Impacts

Why reputation

matters

The casualty rate among CEOs who disregard their role as guardian-in-chief of a company's reputation has never been higher, says David Drobis, Chairman of Ketchum.

Does reputation matter?

I cannot think of a corporate communications officer who would answer that question with anything other than a resounding 'Yes!' But in 2001, many chief executive officers are still weighing the question, unsure if there might be a causal relationship between a damaged reputation and a damaged bottom line.

For some companies, the chance to recognise that relationship has come only with hindsight. Texaco, Salomon Bros., Royal Dutch/Shell, Prudential, Exxon, Mitsubishi – all have suffered because their reputation as good employers, good corporate citizens or good trading partners has been sullied. Books have already been written about many of these companies, each analysing what when wrong and what should have been done. But from where I sit, the answer is depressingly consistent: all of these companies made management decisions in the apparent belief that reputation does not matter, and all have discovered – painfully – that it does.

Reputation matters when consumers boycott a company's products to protest unfair labour practices.

Reputation matters when a company associated with environmental problems is denied approval for a plant expansion.

Reputation matters when a company known for discriminatory practices cannot recruit minority candidates.

Reputation matters – a lot; and the stakes are constantly getting higher. The alienation of a fragment of one's customer base may not seem life threatening. But in today's tempestuous investment climate, anything that is perceived as having a negative impact on earnings can lead to a savage response from shareholders. Witness the inexplicable pummelling of Proctor and Gamble's stock after the company dared to announce that it would only meet analysts' earnings expectations, not exceed them.

Unfortunately, volatility in the stock market is a fact of life that affects all companies at one point or another. What should be of greater concern is the erosion of a company's reputation that can occur when stakeholders start to equate stock price with management competence.

This is not a matter of mere academic interest. A recent *Wall Street Journal* article noted that in the first ten months of 2000, the CEOs of 38 of the 200 largest companies in the US left their posts 'to pursue other interests'. Not only is this 1-in-5 number unprecedented – 'only' 23 *Fortune 200* CEOs were dispatched in 1999 – but also the tenure of these executives has grown shorter and shorter. Boards of Directors are often pressured to make changes at the top after as little as a year.

Yesterday's CEO could sometimes keep corporate missteps behind closed boardroom doors. Not any longer. Today's leader must deal with chat rooms, activist websites and a voracious,

Internet-enabled stakeholder population. Documents intended for internal consumption find their way into the public's hands instantaneously. People and organisations are more connected than ever.

Not only that, but more and more people seem to believe that, with the purchase of one share of a company's stock, they have the right to know everything that happens inside. The US Securities and Exchange Commission appears to agree. The recently-issued Regulation 'Fair Disclosure' affirms that individual investors have the same right to immediate disclosure of material information previously enjoyed by relatively few professional investors and securities analysts. Failure to comply can cost you more than your job – it can land you in jail.

In this increasingly intolerant, high-speed environment, reputation management is not just a nice idea. It has become a basic CEO survival skill.

We *are* talking about survival, for the CEO and often for the company he or she leads. At least for the present, a company's ability to demonstrate that it has the skills and knowledge to thrive in the so-called New Economy has been crucial to attracting investors, employees and customers. Allow your company to be characterised by any of these audiences as a 'legacy' company and you are flirting with disaster.

While we have seen that the mere attachment of 'dotcom' to a company's name is no longer enough to send its stock into space, we have also seen numerous examples of legacy companies that have fallen out of favour as an investment, supplier or employer because their reputation had more in common with buggy whips than e-commerce.

Meanwhile, the globalisation of the economy has added to the complexity of reputation management. A company's reputation travels right along with its business operations, no matter how far flung those operations might be. The lights at headquarters may be out for the day, but the Internet has allowed a company's reputation to be discussed and debated 24 hours a day.

Today, as the personification of a company in the public's mind, the CEO is the chief guardian of a company's reputation.

Fortunately, the majority of CEOs can share this responsibility. In most large companies, the chief public relations or public affairs officer is also in the eye of the storm. It's his or her job to keep track of the full range of issues that have an impact on the reputation of the company. They should have the perspective on every issue and how it affects the various stakeholder groups. Such insight is invaluable to the CEO's decision-making.

That said, we must also realise that corporate reputation is also in the hands of every employee. Each of their actions will be scrutinised by a public waiting to see if the game a company talks is as good as the one it plays. That is why public relations today is far more than just cranking out news releases or staging events. As business communicators, we're more than just cheerleaders and messengers – we are also watchdogs, pollsters, pundits, and, in some cases, institutional psychiatrists. Our job is to help the leadership of a company steer through the countless hazards of our world-as-fishbowl, while helping the company as a whole to understand the vital role reputation plays in achieving the corporate mission.

Because more than ever, reputation is at the heart of business success.

Headquartered in New York, Ketchum, a unit of Omnicom Group Inc. (NYSE: OMC; www.omnicomgroup.com), is the seventh-largest public relations firm in the world with offices and affiliates in key capitals around the globe.

What makes a good corporate reputation

Over half the worth of the world's largest corporations lies in their reputational assets – and those can disappear overnight, unless six rules are followed, says Adrian Wheeler, CEO of GCI UK.

Warner Buffett told Salomon: 'If you lose money I will be understanding. If you lose reputation I will be ruthless.' Investors like Buffett know that a good reputation is the most valuable asset a company possesses.

In today's electronic democracy, a reputation which has taken twenty years to build can be lost overnight. Who would have predicted that companies as venerable as Shell, as popular as McDonald's, as astute as Coca-Cola or as competent as Nike would be injured by reputation catastrophes? *Fortune's* CEOs are right to list corporate reputation as one of their top three personal priorities.

Over half the worth of the world's largest corporations consists of reputational assets – what we used to call 'goodwill'. Good reputation means everything in business. A Hill & Knowlton study by Yankelovitch quantifies the benefits: easier sales, easier recruitment, easier crisis survival, better employee retention, greater pricing power, stronger stock market valuation, better merger/acquisition potential … everything that matters.

There is a direct correlation between corporate reputation and crucial business issues like share-price, regulatory approval, labour relations, community support, retailer preference and consumer support. No one questions that a company's principal purpose is to trade profitably, but nowadays people expect more: they want companies to behave well and to engage their interest on a level over and above the pure commercial transaction.

Yet only 28 per cent of people trust business leaders to tell the truth (MORI), even though 30 per cent of the companies in Yankelovitch's study rewarded CEOs for good corporate reputation stewardship. There is a gulf between the principles which companies espouse and how they actually operate. So what should they do?

At a macro-level it's almost too simple: behave well, make sure that anyone who doesn't leaves immediately, and treat people and organisations with respect and good manners. It is when these rules come into conflict with the threat of an earnings decline or the opportunity for a quick business gain that the company's commitment to best practice is tested. Most falter at this point because the CEO's interests and rewards tend to be short-term, while the interests of the company's other stake-holders are long-term. Most of today's super-brands have been around for decades.

Corporate reputation is a slow-build proposition. It is no accident that an inspirational leader like Richard Branson endows every business he touches with reputational value. Virgin is the most admired and best-loved brand in a multitude of categories – all because of him. People like him and trust him; they have had time to get to know what Branson and Virgin mean. They are engaged by Branson's antics and are inclined to give Virgin the benefit of the doubt. When your planes are delayed and your trains are cancelled, this is a real business benefit.

Most of us inhabit a world where we are not in the headlines every day. We are neither showmen nor conmen, neither Richard Branson nor Marty Frankel. We are doing the best we can to reconcile the apparently conflicting demands of shareholders, employees, customers and regulatory authorities.

I suggest that there is no conflict, provided that the timescale for all stakeholders is the same. Warren Buffet's brilliant insight is that everyone working in a company should fix their attention on developing its long-term reputation – above all else – and should be rewarded or punished accordingly. Here are six components of good corporate reputation, which will win and build intangible value for every kind of firm:

■ **Be obsessed with your product or service:**
However many charities you support, nothing comes close to superior product quality in controlling how people feel about your company. Hewlett-Packard; *The Economist*; Fairy Liquid … they are regarded as simply the best, because the people who make them are obsessed with the product.

■ **Deserve confidence:**
Do your customers and employees really trust you? Do the media see you as a target or as a source of help? Do you and your management team stick to your guns? 'A principle is only a principle when it costs you money.' People expect the captains of today's ships to be first in the lifeboat; you can win incalculable reputation points by putting yourself and your career on the line.

■ **Be available:**
When people complain about a Virgin product, Richard Branson writes to them or rings them up. They are so bowled over that they become Virgin's best advocates. Most senior managers shy away from accessibility: they hire PR people to shield them from the media, IR people to protect them from the city, HR people to intervene with employees, and any number of marketing people to keep customers at a distance. Don't. You are

at the heart of corporate reputation; you should be passionate about your firm's good name and you need to hear what people say, without dilution. Any of IBM's customers can contact Lou Gerstner at any time.

Robert Waterman sums it up in *The Frontiers of Excellence:* 'The key to strategic success is building relationships with customers, suppliers and employees that are exceptionally hard for competitors to duplicate.'

■ Admit mistakes:

Be human. There is a media myth that companies are run by super-beings: it is universal in Germany, prevalent in the UK, going out of style in the US and vestigial in Australia. The media flip their heroes very quickly: one day you are invincible, the next you are dust. Companies are nothing but people; corporate reputations are built by people with vision, talent, beliefs, energy, ambition ... and failings. Let your customers and employees see that you, too, belong to the human race.

■ Engage people's interest:

This is the hardest component to realise, but it is also the factor which distinguishes star performers from the rest. Your company needs a bit of sparkle to lift its reputation out of the ordinary. If you happen to be Richard Branson, Bill Gates or Charles Dunstone, the magic is in your own personality. If you're not ... look for a cause or a crusade which can unite your people and add something to your firm's commercial life, some-thing that will click with your customers and business partners. For British Airways, it's children's charities. For Hasbro, it's raising money for children with leukaemia. Whatever you choose, make sure it's appropriate for your company, and don't just buy it – get everyone personally involved.

■ Have something to say:

Most people think business is boring. Journalists make a huge effort to elicit a point of view – contentious, challenging, sur-prising, individual, different – from the company chiefs that they interview. They find it hard going. Part of corporate reputation is having something to say beyond the facts and figures of your company's performance. Leaders are perceived as people with a consistent agenda which they express colourfully and vigorously. Be an industry pundit or a consumer's champion; be the person who speaks for or against the key industry issue of the day. Most of all, learn how to deliver your viewpoint with impact and personality.

Very few employees think their job is just about making money. Very few customers think that the products they buy regularly are just products. Journalists and analysts, too, are professionally interested in what is really going on in your company. Regulators and governments are swayed by feelings rather than facts. For all these reasons, corporate reputation is the most valuable asset which any company can have – even if it is the least tangible.

Over and above these calculations there is another reason why corporate reputation should be at the top of every CEO's agenda: the extraordinary sense of pride and achievement which you and your colleagues experience when you know your company is truly excellent and is recognised as excellent by the world at large.

Adrian Wheeler co-founded Sterling Public Relations, a financial and corporate consultancy which became GCI London in 1987. He is currently Chief Executive of GCI UK, a top-ten firm with specialist divisions in corporate, consumer, financial, technology and healthcare communications. He advises clients including British Airways, The Royal Mail and the UK toy industry on corporate reputation issues. Wheeler is Chairman of GCI's European Board and Vice-Chairman of the PRCA.

GCI is the youngest of the international public relations firms. Since 1987 it has developed a network of 60 offices worldwide and is currently the fastest-growing PR consultancy in the world. GCI was named 'Agency of the Year' for 1999/2000 by *Inside PR*.

Managing reputation in the internet age

Transparency is the only defence in a world where everyone knows almost everything about you. So why are only 15 per cent of companies actively monitoring their presence on the web, ask Andrew Laurence, Joint Chief Executive, Hill & Knowlton, and Matthew Blakstad, Director, Interactive.

If there was a moment when the dotcoms looked like they might beat traditional business in the race to win the new economy, it passed. In the last two years the 'bricks' have ploughed capital and resources into their e-business transformations, and 2001 shows every sign of being the year when the Empire Strikes Back. However, at least one challenge remains for them. The impact of the Internet on the way companies manage their reputation is as fundamental as it is to every other area of their operations –

business is yet to meet this challenge. According to research Hill & Knowlton carried out with *Chief Executive* magazine last year, only 15 per cent of the companies surveyed monitor their presence on the Internet, and although more than half now have strategies to manage reputation issues in relation to the web – an increase on the previous years findings – three-quarters of CEOs are increasingly concerned about negative information mentioning their firms on the medium.

As cause and catalyst, the net has created a shift in the way corporate reputation is assessed and managed, which fundamentally challenges the way companies communicate. Just as the military provided the original model for managing large organisations, so it was the starting point for the practice of communications. Decisions were usually made in private by a small number of senior officials and communicated on a need-to-know basis. Confidentiality was expected as of right and the watchword for communication was control – of message, medium, recipient and timing. The financial analyst had highest clearance for communications as the prime influence of stockholder and everybody else's opinion. The media, on the other hand, were considered a necessary and occasionally useful evil to be handled with all the care accorded to radioactive material. Clearly there were always exceptions to the model, but many business leaders are discarding these tenets reluctantly.

Companies no longer have control over their communications.

One effect of the Internet is that companies have lost control over their communications. Cyveillance, a Virginia-based web intelligence service, found in a survey of 40 companies that 80 per cent of major brand names are subject to brand abuse on the net. It estimates this costs the average Global 500 company $30 million per year. In a recent search for Nestlé, two of the top five results were highly credible, professional-looking sites criticising the company. One took the form of an official-looking report for the International Baby Food Action Network, while the other was the UK's University of Leicester which was taking a vote on whether to boycott the company alleging irresponsible marketing of breast milk substitutes worldwide.

Companies are under public scrutiny as never before.

Many of the abuses also demonstrate that companies face scrutiny as never before. This is not solely a consequence of the online revolution. The increasing power of a global media, consumer attitudes and a renewed focus on corporate governance have all contributed to this change. Yet the Internet has accelerated the process by allowing anyone with a grievance and sufficient motivation to voice their outrage. There are numerous examples of disgruntled ex-employees establishing rogue sites that criticise their former employers. Similarly, groups of all kinds are using the Internet to promote their concerns with corporate behaviour. Consumer activist sites such as www.untied.com, which highlights service issues at United Airlines, have proved litigation proof because they represent the real concerns of customers rather than the opinion of the publishers. Established activist groups are the most sophisticated and experienced users of the Internet as a campaigning tool. In the UK, Greenpeace publishes a site that allows consumers to consult pollution league tables and identify the major polluters within their area. Internationally, the same organisation recently mounted a campaign to attack Coca-Cola's use of CFCs using imagery drawn from the company's logo, colours, Olympic sponsorship and advertising campaign. The www.McSpotlight site has kept up a four-year war against McDonalds, while the Boycott Board and other sites regularly 'out' a variety of companies for abuse of customers, the environment and human rights. The Internet enables activist groups worldwide to band together to organise and publicise global protests such as the 'Battle in Seattle' last year, as well as select corporations to pillory along the way.

Their toolkit includes a bewildering array of aggressive tactics such as encouraging users to bombard companies with messages, overloading their communications teams and sometimes their systems. Pyramid protest if you like.

The Internet's speed, reach and interactivity creates new opportunities for dialogue and relationships with stakeholders.

The Internet is vast and fast. Research company Jupiter predicts 80 per cent penetration of US households by 2005, and finds time spent online by users to be half that spent watching TV and rising. The 'I Love You' virus proved a message can reach and affect the world almost immediately. More recently, a lawyer in leading UK law firm Norton Rose forwarded an indiscreet e-mail from a girlfriend to six colleagues. Within a few days it had been forwarded to millions and appeared as a news story on three continents causing embarrassment to all concerned. (This accidental mass communication also evidences a new loss of control for companies as e-mail and the Internet blur the lines between internal and external communication. Add the spectre of declining loyalty amongst employees and damaging leaks may become a common phenomenon.)

Speed is often the deciding factor for whether a company succeeds in the new economy. So it is with communication. The first to communicate often has the edge. Companies now have the opportunity and obligation (in a crisis) to communicate as rapidly and specifically as time allows.

As it is instantaneous, the medium also offers the opportunity for interaction. The traditional model for corporate communication is a single message pushed in a variety of ways at an audience. While many companies lay claim to building meaningful relationships with stakeholders, our experience is that communications with all interest groups apart from the financial community tends predominately to be one-way and transactional.

Also, until recently a relatively small proportion of companies have made inroads into segmentation of their messages by stakeholder interest. The Internet allows communicators to think in terms of conversations rather than messages, the specific needs of target groups and relationships rather than transactions. With its reputation burned by the Brent Spa debacle, Shell undertook a massive and open dialogue with its stakeholders about its business activities and ethics. Social reporting, Internet sites, press relations and publications were all employed to this end. They also committed to building real relationships with activists and other interested parties for the first time. This refocusing around listening was a first for Shell and their image appears to be improving as a result.

Big business rises to the challenge

The most reluctant of companies are sufficiently impressed by the risks and opportunities of the Internet to test the water. Some have become vigilant, using technology to monitor what is said about them on the web. At Hill & Knowlton we have a product Radar, which employs natural language technology to search and filter issues as well as keywords. Others have hired 'cybernauts' to patrol their web image. For some companies this will throw up huge amounts of information and the art will be to select which ground to defend. Companies are also learning practical strategies for dealing with Internet attacks. The most successful are those that temper the desire for control with transparency and interaction. For example, when Volkswagen threatened to sue Beetle affinity groups for trademark infringements, they turned hundreds of potential advocates into critics. On the other hand, when Dunkin Donuts sponsored a critic site and made it central to their approach to customer service, they turned damage to advantage. Companies including Monsanto, Shell and P&G have created microsites to respond to specific issues of concern to customers or stakeholders. In the area of crisis response, where time is most critical, extranet sites are increasingly vital to an effective crisis response. A click through icon appeared on the Air France website within an hour of last year's Concorde crash, routing traffic to a dedicated contact point.

There is one area where companies can retain a degree of control over communication. Disintermediation of the media means news and information sources are proliferating, and a new breed of Internet journalist is emerging, often without the credibility of a 'branded' news media source backing them. Research by US web consultancy Middleberg & Associates suggests media in the US are increasingly likely to use the Internet as a primary research tool and consult company websites. This offers companies an opportunity to create credible sources of news and information on their companies and relevant issues that allows them to get a controlled message into the hands of the public.

Far-sighted companies are seeing beyond these essentially defensive strategies, recognising the opportunity to build their brand reputation and meaningful relationships with customers and other stakeholders by creating online communities of interest. Roche created one of the first sites to provide definitive information for HIV sufferers and professionals, demonstrating their clear leadership in the field. Companies like Heineken and Warner Brothers provide platforms or downloads of branding and materials for affinity groups to create their own sites within the context of the brand. BT created a Global Information Exchange – an executives lounge where telecom professionals can chat and debate as well as search news and library facilities. Even Amazon.com can be seen as a community as well as a commercial enterprise.

Several factors are emerging for a corporate sponsored community to succeed – it must host an issue of burning interest, where the sponsor has credibility; content must be rich; and it must be interactive, entertaining or deeply informative and easy to access.

There is another aspect to these online communities – the most powerful are the new intermediaries and opinion setters in the online world. BioMedNet has become the world's largest community of biochemistry and medical professionals; GeoCities is a virtual community in every sense – you even choose the neighbourhood where you intend to live – and is now beginning to offer a commercial dimension. These communities, like real-world communities, carry influence with their members. Their endorsement of a brand or company may enhance its credibility and sales. Mapping and devising strategies to build relationships with relevant online communities will be central to effective corporate and marketing communication in the future.

Rewriting the rules of reputation

The direct impact of the Internet on corporate communication may be impressive, but it is as a catalyst for redrawing the rules of reputation that its effect may be greatest.

Good corporate citizenship is moving from 'nice to do' to 'must do'. There have always been companies that have believed they should make a positive net contribution to the communities in which they operate – Johnson & Johnson is a fine example of a company that enshrined this belief in a credo, set down in 1949, and lives by it. Corporate America generally has a good record of giving – the huge foundations of McDonalds and other traditional companies, and the efforts of newer companies like Microsoft and Cisco, set standards for other markets where corporate philanthropy is less overt or advanced.

However, research and pundits suggest an even more fundamental contribution to society will be expected in the future. There is a wealth of data that says employees and consumers have higher expectations of companies than ever before. Taking responsibility for the side effects of their operations, environmental or otherwise, is taken as read. Yet, research in the US (Yankelovich) and the UK (Henley Centre) suggests that consumers want to see companies go further and contribute to the resolution of the big issues facing the societies and governments in which they operate: health, education, crime, poverty and the digital divide. Research amongst employees conducted by Cone/Roper in 1999 shows that staff prefer to work for companies that take these issues seriously and act upon them. The Internet has enabled all who would make companies more accountable for their actions to exert pressure in a way they could not have done before.

Second, transparency is the only defence in a world where everyone knows almost everything about you. The Henley Centre research shows trust in big companies and other sources of authority continues to decline, and UK market research firm MORI found that only a quarter of people feel that big business profits are a good thing. In an age where trust is harder to win, consumers are more sophisticated, sceptical and demanding than ever and where the media and Internet have unparalleled power to challenge corporate behaviour, companies have no choice but to be more open about every aspect of their behaviour. Like Shell, they may occasionally still make an unpopular decision on commercial grounds, but they have to be open to explaining it.

The trends towards transparency and accountability were in progress before the Internet – but the online revolution has played a vital role in accelerating them and has probably made them irreversible. It could be argued that corporate behaviour is being humanised and, to an extent, democratised in the new economy. The global community is demanding that companies are honest, transparent, live by values, build meaningful relationships, and take responsibility in their communities. It would be ironic if a technology proved to be the force that makes them human.

Hill & Knowlton are one of the world's largest international public relations consultancies with 70 offices in 34 countries. The company represents 60 per cent of the Fortune 500.

Andrew Laurence is Joint Chief Executive of Hill & Knowlton UK and leads the companies European Corporate Practice. Matthew Blakstad is Head of the Interactive Practice in the UK.

Reputation's return on investment

PR is best measured by increased sales, employee retention and a stable investor base, not by media impressions or message content, says Jack Bergen at the US Council of PR Firms. He reviews the ways in which the full strategic value of a company's intangible assets can currently be established.

The public relations profession has a golden opportunity to reinforce the strategic importance of its work to business performance and market valuation. Spurred by recognition of the value of intellectual capital in the modern corporation, business economists and accounting firms are beginning to address how to put a value on 'intangible assets'. Even securities analysts in a study conducted by Ernst & Young said that 30 to 50 per cent of the valuations they place on a company are based on non-financial factors. The media is also picking up the mantra:

> *The value of a business increasingly lurks not in physical and financial assets that are on the balance sheet, but in intangibles.* (*The Economist*, 12 June 1999)

While others are only now recognising the value of non-financial assets, public relations has always emphasised the importance of such intangibles as employee commitment, customer confidence, brand loyalty, management credibility and public trust. These are corporate assets that public relations has been building and protecting for decades. Today we often refer to that important public relations effort as reputation management, using the term reputation to represent the sum of those intangible assets.

If we agree that reputation is a corporate asset and that public relations is the steward of corporate reputation, it is important to make that case in the language and analysis acceptable to those who claim to guard the integrity of corporate valuations and assets – business economists and professors, accounting firms and CFOs. Measuring public relations outputs like media impressions or message content won't cut it. We need to determine business outcomes of our work – increased sales, employee retention and stable investor base. We need to base our case for resources not on press clips but on the return on investment (ROI) of public relations.

The Council of Public Relations Firms, the trade association representing the US public relations industry, has undertaken several studies to address the need for methodologies that meet the 'Cynical CFO Test'. The most ambitious is our development of a methodology to predict and measure business outcomes of public relations programmes. This effort will undoubtedly take several years and we may well find that public relations is more an art than a science – therefore outcomes cannot be predicted. We have just completed a study that identified the essential elements of corporate reputation and reviewed the existing measurement protocols for tracking reputation. However, the study that provides the foundation for public relations' role in corporate reputation is most relevant to this book.

In early 1999, the newly-formed Council was looking for a way to demonstrate convincingly to non-communications business executives what every public relations person knows intuitively – that public relations is a strategic business tool that impacts a company's competitive success and financial returns. The increasing focus on intangibles and corporate reputation offered just such an opportunity. In March, *CEO Magazine* published a survey conducted by Yankleovitch and sponsored by Hill & Knowlton that found that 96 per cent of CEOs believed their company's reputation was vital to business success, including 77 per cent who felt it affected sales of products and services. Burson Marsteller had been doing similar analysis with the research firm Wirthlin Worldwide, surveying a broader group of business and media audiences. Those polls had a strong impact on our profession, but they were based on opinions about the link between reputation and business returns, lacking tangible correlations to win over cynical CFOs. Nor did they address directly the link between public relations and corporate reputation that the Council sought to demonstrate. Finally, they lacked the national acceptance and high visibility on which to build a base for a major awareness campaign.

Fortune magazine's 'most admired companies' ranking seemed to address two of those needs. It is a high profile and universally acknowledged measure of reputation that has built acceptance during 18 years of rankings. A high standing on the list was often used as an identifier for a company, as 'a top ten most admired company,' even by other publications. In its discussion of the rankings, *Fortune* also emphasised the correlation between standing on the list and financial returns. A chart accompanying the 1999 list showed that *Fortune's* top ten most admired companies had returns of 70.5 per cent, versus 27.1 per cent for the S&P average and −26.8 per cent for the ten least admired. So *Fortune* helped to make the connection between reputation and results.

The Council decided to test the 1999 *Fortune* rankings to connect the final link – between public relations and reputation. We decided to determine if public relations played a part in the standings. Polling a representative sample of 120 of the 476 US corporations ranked, we asked not for their opinions, but for their budgets. We decided to see if the size of investment in corporate communications correlated with standings in reputation. As Figure 1.4.1 shows, there appears to be a strong correlation throughout each quintile of the *Fortune* ranking.

The analysis considers the traditional functions supervised by the corporate communications officer: media relations, executive outreach and speechwriting, investor relations, quarterly and annual reports, employee communications, industry relations, corporate and issues advertising, foundation and philanthropy programmes, community relations and department management functions. It does not include marketing public relations, which is usually managed by business units. Since the budget is heavily weighted by corporate and issues advertising and foundation and philanthropy programmes, we simplified the analysis by eliminating those programmes and comparing the top 200 reputation companies to the bottom 200 (Figure 1.4.2). The difference is dramatic, with 'reputation haves' spending more than twice as much as 'reputation have-nots' on corporate communications.

Looking at the budgets of the separate functional areas gives us a sense of which functions have the greatest impact on reputation (Figure 1.4.3). The most dramatic difference between the spending

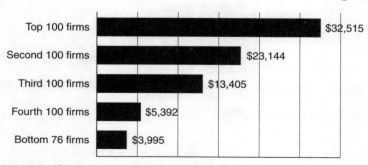

Fig. 1.4.1: Budgets of 120 US corporations

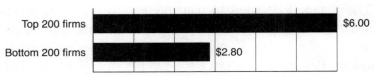

Fig. 1.4.2: Comparison between top and bottom firms

of 'haves' and 'have-nots' occurred in employee communications budgets. This seems to affirm the intuition of many public relations officers that they can get the greatest reputation leverage with all stakeholders through their employees. It stands to reason. Employees certainly are on the front line with customers, whether they are directly interacting in service industries or affecting the quality of the products they assemble and craft. In the highly competitive talent marketplace, employees' views dominate, influencing productivity, recruiting and retention. They are the face of the company in the community. With the proliferation of employee 401K and other stock plans, employees and retirees are a growing – and increasingly vocal – investor force.

In testing whether company size could be affecting the correlation between budgets and reputation, the Council also analysed the proportion of total company revenue spent on corporate communications (Figure 1.4.4). We found that the correlations continued to hold

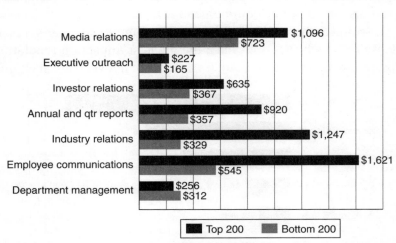

Fig. 1.4.3: Budgets of separate functional areas

true, with the highest reputation companies spending proportionally more on corporate communications at each quintile level. What was most illuminating – and shocking – in this analysis is the relatively small amount of a corporation's total budget spent on those functions that enhance its reputation with its key stakeholders, influencers and the media. While it may not be surprising that the companies with the worst reputation spend about one-twentieth of one per cent on corporate communications, it is surprising that even the top reputation companies only dedicate one-fifth of one per cent of their total revenues on corporate communications.

Public relations professionals cannot fight the resource and reputation battle alone. The Council is encouraging third parties to enter the fray. For example, we are supporting the efforts of other publications to build credibility for their measures of reputation. While *Fortune* magazine has the most prominence, it is a flawed measure because it only polls corporate officers and directors and securities analysts within individual industry sectors. That misses other key stakeholders – customers, employees, government officials and the media. In addition to the *CEO Magazine* poll, the Council and its members have directly supported, in co-operation with reputation guru Charles Fombrun and Harris Interactive, the development of a multi-stakeholder reputation ranking by the *Wall Street Journal*. In addition, the Council has been collaborating with PriceWaterhouseCoopers, which helps the *Financial Times* conduct its annual 'World's Most Respected Companies' ranking.

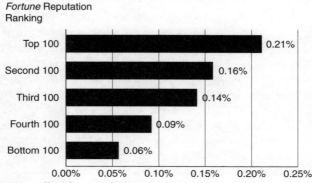

Fig. 1.4.4: Spending by total revenue

Rankings help to build awareness for the importance of reputation, but sceptics will rightly point out that they are the business media's own publicity stunts, created partly to increase corporate advertising sales for the publications. We believe that the credibility of corporate reputation and public relations' role in building and preserving reputation depends on solid research. For that reason, the Council recently commissioned a review of nine research measurement protocols offered by commercial research firms. Assessing them by a variety of criteria – from cost to customisation – the review provides a guide to those who are searching for a way to plan and measure their reputation management programmes. The Council will update the guide on a quarterly basis, considering the success with the different protocols and adding new reviews as research firms introduce new reputation planning and measurement products.

Encouraging the research industry, and the management consulting and software firms that are developing reputation assurance and reputation risk management products, will increase the awareness and acceptance of the entire category of reputation management. It will also raise the competitive value of the services provided by public relations firms and enhance respect for the importance of the corporate public relations officer's role in managing that critical asset of the enterprise. The field of reputation management holds the key to the renaissance of public relations.

Representing 125 of the top public relations firms in the US, the Council of Public Relations Firms is the trade association for the American PR industry. The Council seeks to build an understanding of the value of public relations as a strategic business tool with non-communications business executives, potential recruits and the business media. Jack Bergen, the first president of the three-year-old Council, is a former CEO of GCI Group, the PR arm of Grey Global Group. Mr. Bergen also served at GE, Westinghouse and CBS, where he was the senior vice president of corporate relations, responsible for all public relations, government affairs and investor communications.

Measuring reputation

Weber Shandwick Worldwide has invested in a global initiative to create a systematic approach to reputation measurement and evaluation. Chris Genasi, Chief Executive Corporate, reviews the six factors which make or break corporate reputations.

One of the strangest sights in PR is to see highly experienced, confident and accomplished PR practitioners appear to lose their professional composure as soon as the subject of measurement and evaluation arises.

One minute they are skilfully piloting the reputation of a major corporation, the next they are behaving like PR graduates, all because someone has asked the question – 'how are we going to measure the effectiveness of our communications programme?'.

What is it about evaluation and measurement which seems to so debilitate even the most experienced of practitioners? The problem seems to be exacerbated by the misconception that there is an 'agreed' way to evaluate PR and that it is essential to discover that model and apply it. This view is no doubt fuelled by experience in advertising where a common currency of Gross Rating Points etc has developed.

Of course in PR we do things differently – evaluation is more complex and reflects the diversity of our industry. Unlike advertising, PR has no commonly agreed measurement and evaluation protocols. However, this is something that should be celebrated rather than putting us off the idea of measurement and evaluation altogether.

Those who claim that 'you can't measure PR' due to these lack of agreed evaluation standards are selling themselves and the whole PR profession short. By never trying to measure – however imperfectly – PR is denying itself the ability to put down roots in an organisation. Without evaluation there are no benchmarks, no way of knowing if progress is being made, no accountability; therefore, the value of PR is at best unclear, at worst invisible – and therefore dispensable.

Clearly it is time for the PR industry to stop moaning and start measuring. But how?

This article will focus on measuring reputation. There are many other areas that require measurement and evaluation, but arguably these are well-documented and a range of evaluation companies have sprung up to help the PR practitioner track areas such as media coverage.

However, measuring and tracking the reputation of an organisation or a brand is an area where very little has been written and where very few companies are providing a specific service.

How does a company go about measuring and evaluating its reputation?

There are three levels of knowledge that an organisation needs to equip itself with before it is able to measure and track its reputation:

Level 1:	**Who matters?** ■ With which audiences do you want to have a good reputation?
Level 2:	**What matters?** ■ What attributes do audiences take into account when considering the reputation of companies in general – what matters to them? ■ Sector relevance – what factors matter specifically in your industry sector? For example, big reputational issues for a chemical manufacturer will be very different from those of a retailer. ■ Your priorities – what aspects of your specific company's reputation are you interested in? What key messages about your reputation are you keen to stress and promote?
Level 3:	**Measurement matters** ■ What do you want your reputation to be? ■ How will you know if your reputation has changed? ■ How will you know what factors have led to that change in reputation?

Because of the lack of research or knowledge in the area of measuring corporate reputation, Weber Shandwick Worldwide has invested in the first global initiative to create a systematic approach to reputation measurement and evaluation.

A few years ago, Weber Shandwick Worldwide approached Professor Charles Fombrun of the Stearn Business School at New York University, one of the world's foremost experts on corporate reputation. With Professor Fombrun, Weber Shandwick Worldwide embarked on a major reputation research project, the aim of which was to find out which factors people considered important when forming a view of the reputation of a corporation. The study also sought to find out which corporations had the best and the worst reputations in the world and to track their progress over time to see how reputation might affect their business performance.

This led to one of the biggest studies of its kind. Over 12,000 individuals, from members of the public to opinion formers, were included in online surveys carried out by Harris Research in the US. The research will soon be carried out across six European countries.

The result was the birth of the Reputation Quotient (RQ) – the world's first rating to measure corporate reputation. This research allows companies to put a rating on their reputation, to see how they fare against competitors and peers and to let them track the progress of their 'reputation equity' over time.

Weber Shandwick Worldwide does not want to keep the RQ to itself. The aim is to develop the RQ into a universal measure for reputation that can become a global standard. Eventually we hope that the RQ will become as transferable and as widely understood a currency as measurements of temperature, speed, share price, or even shoe size.

So what is the RQ index? The Shandwick/Fombrun research showed that respondents considered around 20 key factors when forming a view on a company's reputation. Professor Fombrun then clustered these factors into six drivers of reputation: emotional appeal, products and services, workplace environment, vision and leadership, social responsibility and financial performance. Figure 1.5.1 shows the characteristics of each of the six reputation drivers.

With the reputation drivers established as the criteria for measuring corporate reputation for companies in general, the next task was to ask respondents to score a range of corporations against each driver on a simple scoring scale. This creates a reputation scorecard for individual companies, which can be used to set goals, and to track progress.

Scores for each driver are then averaged, producing the RQ for that company. The reputation scorecard can then be extended to include important measures relevant to that particular industry sector as well as specific messages or themes

Attributes and Drivers

Fig. 1.5.1: Characteristics of six reputation drivers

relevant to an individual company. An example of such a reputation scorecard is shown below:

Reputation Score (where 1 = poor and 6 = excellent)

	1	2	3	4	5	6
General reputation driver						
Emotional appeal		X				
Products and services			X			
Workplace environment		X				
Vision and leadership			X			
Social responsibility				X		
Financial performance				X		
Sector specific reputation drivers						
Sustainable use of water			X			
Fair prices	X					
Reputation drivers specific to this company						
Innovative new products	X					
Committed to local economy				X		
Developing new markets				X		

The RQ for this company is 2.82, based on an average of all the scores given above.

Reputation scorecards can be developed for individual audience groups, to show variations. Also, competitor scoring can be overlayed to provide a context. In addition, 'best and worst in class' companies can be added to the scorecard to benchmark your corporate reputation against a full spectrum.

Another useful aspect of developing a reputation scorecard is that 'stretch targets' against business goals can be set. This allows communications professionals to set targets and measure progress over time. For example, a target could be set to improve reputation scores by one point within 18 months. In some cases the target could be to reduce a score. For example, a company may wish to lower its profile in a certain area to allow other sides of the business to have an airing. A sample reputation scorecard is shown below with actual and target ratings:

Reputation Score (where 1 = poor and 6 = excellent)

	1	2	3	4	5	6
General reputation driver						
Emotional appeal		X		O		
Products and services			XO			
Workplace environment		X	O			
Vision and leadership			X		O	
Social responsibility				XO		
Financial performance				XO		
Sector specific reputation drivers						
Sustainable use of water			XO			
Fair prices	X		O			
Reputation drivers specific to this company						
Innovative new products	X				O	
Committed to local economy				XO		
Developing new markets		O		X		

X= actual rating; O = target rating in 18 months time

As can be seen this company aims to move its overall RQ from 2.82 to 3.64, based on the average actual and target ratings shown above.

Having a better understanding of your company's reputational strengths and weaknesses vs your competitors and then setting measurable goals to address those issues, provides a rational basis to develop a corporate reputation management programme.

This process creates a clear set of priorities, identifies a well-signposted reputation road map and provides a mechanic to measure progress on that journey. This transforms PR – perhaps for the first time in many organisations – into a strategic, measurable and accountable business discipline that contributes towards helping a business achieve its goals.

So how does a company go about measuring these factors? The optimal route is to use independent audience research. Any reputable research company will advise on the process for conducting research with your target audience. Another option is to consider joining one of the several omnibus surveys of corporate audiences, although the cost of this can often be comparable to a bespoke survey on corporate reputation.

Another option is to evaluate media coverage and to transpose the content of the coverage onto the reputation scorecards. The basis being that what has been covered in the media is likely to be reflective of current thinking about your company's reputation and that of your competitors.

While this is better than no evaluation at all, the limitation is that media evaluation focuses only on the outcome of PR activity in the media, it does not track out-take of the coverage in terms of how the coverage has influenced the behaviour and attitudes of the target audiences. Media evaluation also does not measure the impact of non-media activity, which can be significant in many reputation management campaigns.

The expense of full audience research need not be prohibitive. The Institute of Public Relations and the Public Relations Consultants Association in their guidelines on research, measurement and evaluation suggest the following levels of spend on measurement and evaluation:

Budget (£)	% to Measurement	
	Minimum	**Optimum**
Up to 50,000	10	12
50–100,000	7	10
100–500,000	5	7
500,000 +	3	5

By following these guidelines, most major corporations should be able to afford a formal audience research assignment and/or media evaluation at least once every 18 months.

By making this commitment, the reputation management team will be equipped to take their place with pride alongside the other professional disciples at the boardroom table.

Chris Genasi has over 14 years experience of public relations. His specialism is the management of corporate reputation and he has advised several leading multinational companies including Nestlé, Lever Brothers, Toyota Motor Corporation, Castrol, BP, Allied Domecq, Courtaulds Fibres, Rolls-Royce Motor Cars and BT.

At Weber Shandwick Worldwide he is responsible for the company's Corporate Division. Chris has particular expertise in: communications strategy development, internal culture change programmes, issues management, corporate media relations, opinion former communications and corporate citizenship activity.

Chris began his career in market research before moving into PR consultancy and retains a strong interest in the use of research and evaluation in PR. He is a member of the Account Planning Group, the International Association of Business Communicators, The Institute of Social and Ethical Accountability and the Institute of Public Relation's City and Financial Group. He also sits on the Consultancy Management Committee of the Public Relations Consultants Association, as well as the Corporate Responsibility Group and The Council of the Institute of Public Relations.

Chris is the author of *Corporate Community Investment*, the first book to provide a practical model for effective business investment in community relations and cause-related marketing.

2

Expectations

Global campaigns & communications

Global reputations are being made and broken by new rules, says Graham Lancaster, Chairman, Biss Lancaster Euro RSCG.

Global communication poses considerable challenges to those charged with managing the corporate reputations of major businesses and institutions. Wire services, broadcasters, the financial markets and the Internet can carry news and views instantaneously around the world and the old rules of public relations have had to be rewritten. This is PR in real time, and a firm's market capital can be on the line. So can careers. Considered, committee-written responses to news inquiries have to be replaced with scenario planning. Early warning systems need to be in place. Reactions to the predictable need to be role-played. Rebuttal policies even on unlikely situations also have to be worked on. Instantaneous media demands instantaneous responses, and for this, key people need to live and breathe the company. It is a relentless and unfor-giving 24/7 process. For the modern PR professional the message is blunt – it's add value, or it's adios.

If this high wire act were not tough enough, corporate reputa-tions are notoriously hard to pin down, manage and measure. They have been described as being the subjective, derivative and collective assessment of the trustworthiness and reliability of firms. Consider those words – subjective, derivative and collective – all painfully difficult concepts, making reputation management appear to many hard-nosed, data-driven CEOs as the last remaining black art of business.

Here is a good definition from Fombrun and Rindova, but it illustrates the challenge to the subscribers to the 'if you can't measure it you can't manage it' school of thought:

> *A corporate reputation is a collective representation of a firm's past actions and results that describe the firm's ability to deliver valued outcomes to multiple stake-holders. It gauges a firm's relative standing both inter-nally with employees and externally with its stakeholders, in both its competitive and institutional environments.*

Here's another angle from *Corporate Reputation Review* on how sociologists see the issue:

> *As indicators of legitimacy: aggregate assessments of a firm's performance relative to expectations and norms in an institutional field.*

When international considerations are also stirred into this particular cauldron, the practical day-to-day business of reputation management becomes very challenging indeed. Research conducted by the International Committee of the UK's Public Relations Consultants' Association amongst clients identified some key barriers to successful international PR campaigns. The top three concerns were the communications processes to be used, the provision of good briefing and securing local expertise. These are very practical issues. As were the key elements for international co-ordination. The top three here were project management, languages and conflict between local and central management.

It is clear from this that there is uncertainty and a real lack of confidence in this whole area of briefing, managing and measuring international campaigns. Confusion conceptually, as well as confusion on how to do it at an operational level. Confusion and uncertainty is fertile soil for providers of consultancy services. Company management teams are rightly risk averse when it comes to vital activities such as international reputation management and crisis PR. Neither is a time to find yourself on a learning curve and so experienced heads are always in demand. It should also be fertile ground for more academics, management schools and business trainers where generally I believe more faculty time and expertise should be found. The Reputation Institute is one organisation very active in this area, however, and their website is invaluable (www.reputationinstitute.com).

Here are some tips on the priorities and options faced by corporations in managing international corporate reputations.

First there is the need to understand the image and reputation you and your competitors currently have amongst the various key audiences in the various countries important to you. Equally important is to understand the reputation of the sector or sectors you are perceived to be in, as that is a major driver of corporate reputations. London based research company MORI, for example, have pioneered a methodology of auditing reputations amongst captains of industry, target journalists, politicians and others based on the interaction of how familiar your sector and, separately, your company is alongside how favourably you are viewed. This is tracked regularly alongside named competitors and other major corporations with which you may want to be benchmarked.

This kind of intelligence is needed prior to tackling the main task – that of agreeing the corporate positioning you actually want to project internally and externally. One factor that may come in to play as you address this could be the issue of national stereotyping. Just as you will be pigeon-holed with all the baggage of your sector – pharmaceuticals, engineering, retail etc – you may also find yourself pigeon-holed as American, German, Norwegian, French or whatever. While most US-rooted multi-nationals prefer to be seen as global/international and not American, few really achieve this, no matter how much of their production is located overseas.

This is a generally under-researched area, although the European Commission has financed work on transnational communication in Europe through the Freie Universitat Berlin. Professor Morosini at IMD in Lausanne has also conducted some very interesting empirical work which looks at national cultural differences, plotted against degrees of conservatism and of hierarchical cultures: this has Denmark, for example, on a low hierarchical and low conservative rating through to Mexico, towards the opposite end of the spectrum.

Some firms deliberately emphasise their country of origin, and leverage positive aspects of national stereotyping. So we have had years of Marlboro Man as an idealised image of America; engineering excellence from German car firms (like Audi's Vorsprung durch Technik); chic from France (Renault's 'Papa and Nicole'); Swedish eccentricity (IKEA); Scottish thrift (Scottish Widows); Australian manliness (Castlemaine XXXX); and P J O'Rourke teasing about 'Britishness' for British Airways.

Other key considerations are the degree to which your international PR should be centrally controlled. This is itself a cultural issue, not just one of managerial tidiness. A highly centralised command and control approach, with little local market autonomy, is one extreme; an approach largely devolved to local markets is the other. Most solutions are some way in-between, but all will need that crystal clear agreed positioning, proper funding and resource allocation commensurate with the importance of corporate reputation, and pre-agreed benchmarks for measuring and evaluating results.

Graham Lancaster is Chairman of Biss Lancaster Euro RSCG, one of the UK's leading PR consultancies which he co-founded in 1978. He began his career in production management with Hawker Siddeley Aviation and clothing manufacturer, Corah, before joining the Confederation of British Industry where he became Policy Co-ordinator to the President. Graham was voted Pathfinders' 'Media Boss of the Year' for 2000/1, and is Chairman of the Public Relations Consultants Association from 2002. He is a member of the Governing Council of the CBI and a regular speaker and broadcaster on a range of communications issues. His main outside interest is writing, having published six books (four of them spy thrillers). *The 20 per cent Factor*, a management self-help book published by Kogan Page, has become an international bestseller.

Consumers' contradictory expectations

In an age of global retailing, consumers can afford to be strong-willed and contradictory, say Ira Matathia and Marian Salzman at The Intelligence Factory.

In Europe, the barriers that have held the markets hostage for so long are tumbling down. One can barely keep pace with the headlines: frantic deregulation, rapid-fire mergers and acquisitions across industries, and a seeming explosion of advanced connective technologies related to the Internet, including WAP-equipped mobile phones, televisions and even game consoles. If brands are nothing more nor less than identities, then today's Europe the brand is like nothing we have read about in the history books.

Europe the brand

As the European Union solidifies, its nations are showing a greater determination to respond affirmatively to American cultural and economic expansionism. Individually and together, European nations are 'rebranding' themselves, emphasising the power of the past together with unique national innovations. Scotland has even gone so far as to appoint an 'ambassador' for Scotland the brand – to promote such Scottish qualities as integrity, inventiveness, tenacity and independence of spirit – in the hope that people will buy Scottish goods as the result of automatically equating them with these values.

Despite all the talk of privatisation and deregulation, there is an upside to Europe's steadfast faith in public-private partnerships. Particularly in a rapidly emerging techconomy, regionally harmonised telecom standards and the ability to target and superfund industry innovation are two major pluses. These factors help explain why and how Europe is fast becoming identified with consumer technologies on the edge, such as the Internet-connected mobile phone and the memory-laden 'smart card'.

The new consumerism

In this rapidly-changing climate, one thing is certain: the next decade will indeed be the decade of global retailing. Thanks to the steady resurgence of consumer markets, the coming global middle class will total nearly 2 billion. But they will not simply buy whatever we try to sell them. The passive consumer has been made extinct as technology and cheap labour have shifted global capitalism from worries about production to the frantic push for consumption. In an environment where everyone is competing for the consumer's attention, one cannot impose one's vision of anything.

Moreover, consumers are highly sophisticated today, having viewed advertising virtually from birth, on billboards, TV, the tops of cars and sides of buses, the tabletops of cafes, and so on.

Adding to their power is the fact that universal Internet access is not far off, eventually affording every individual nearly limitless access to information. According to market research company International Data Corp., 'By the end of 2001, there will be more people online in Europe than in the US…Europe is already ahead in mobile-phone use, and by 2003, Europeans accessing the Internet by cell phone will outnumber Americans by nearly two to one.'

Shoppers today know that the market needs them more than they need a particular retailer. They therefore feel free to walk into IKEA or Zara and say rather openly, 'What's in it for me? And while we're at it, what's your company doing to help the planet?' This is not to suggest that today's consumers are immune to the lure of the product. We're all as greedy and self-indulgent as ever. But it does mean increased demand for individualised products, services, and even marketing efforts. It also means that tomorrow's brands will only exist interactively.

From consumer to prosumer

The Intelligence Factory calls the new consumers 'prosumers', as in proactive consumers. They are liberated shoppers, but their lives are highly contradictory, and the challenge is for brands to effectively reconcile their opposing demands.

The first contradiction? Prosumers have lots of cash to spend but no time to shop – they're too busy working. Verdict Research, in the UK, comments that such a shopper will 'resent every moment spent in the retail scrum'. In a time-pressed, information-overloaded society, any product or service that simplifies life will be a valued resource. Popular brands will be those that go the extra mile to remove 'time stress' from the shopping experience, by staying open 24/7, offering home delivery, and so on.

Second, prosumers are serious about value and refuse to spend more than what they think something is worth. But then again, if the prosumer wants something, then money is no object. In

Britain, for instance, the rich are coming up with new and ever more offbeat ways to spend their money. Jeweller Theo Fennell sells a solid-silver Viagra holder. Pear Tree offers a £20,000 custom-made tree house that seats 35, complete with electricity and a kitchen with hot and cold running water, a stove and a bar. Burberry is opening up a whole arena of useless consumerism, ranging from dog coats to designer eye masks – for those tiring, long-haul first-class flights.

The third contradiction in prosumer behaviour is that they latch onto trends easily and quickly, but are fickle and get bored just as fast. New becomes old nearly as soon as it hits the shelf.

Fourth, prosumers are spontaneous and whimsical, yet at the same time socially aware. They will buy a brand that is associated with progressive causes. Of the more than 2 million customers of the Co-operative Bank, based in Manchester, England, 38 per cent claim that the main reason they chose the bank was because of its ethics; for example, Co-operative won't lend to companies directly involved in extracting fossil fuels. The bank has opened a National Centre for Business and Ecology to advise its customers on how to make their own businesses greener, and has partnered with Greenpeace to introduce a biodegradable credit card. However, a cause is no substitute for identity; people will buy in only if the product is already perceived as 'happening' or 'quality'.

Finally, although prosumers themselves would like to escape the constant demands of society – ringing cellphone, beeper, information invasion via CNN and the like – they insist that retailers provide them with personalised customer service on a 'round-the-clock basis'. Yet the power of a solid brand engenders sufficient trust that customers will allow multiple kinds of responsiveness – for example, an e-mail from customer service – as long as the response is quick and personalised. The one thing they will not forgive, however, is obvious insincerity. It is not enough for a brand to seem to care; taking real responsibility is a must.

The Intelligence Factory (IF) is an independent company within Y&R Inc., the worldwide marketing communications company. IF's mandate is to serve as the knowledge company within Y&R, creating products and services that spur employee and client thinking on issues, trends and events affecting consumer markets worldwide.

Ira Matathia, CEO, is former CEO of Chiat/Day Toronto and Chiat/Day New York, and former CEO of TBWA Italia and TBWA International's Department of the Future.

Marian Salzman, Worldwide Director, is author of a dozen books and a pioneer in the field of online research. Her passion for market research and consumer insights has earned her a position as one of the world's leading trendspotters.

See www.intelligencefactory.com

Managing the pressure

How should companies handle a battering from pressure groups or anti-corporate activists? asks Sara Render, Chief Executive of Kinross & Render. First, identify the ethical principles that underpin the company and measure those against stakeholder expectations. Then engage in constructive dialogue. And at all costs, avoid the tactics of Goliath.

A company's reputation is built by the quality of its products or services, its communications, its marketing and last, but not least, its conduct. The management of reputation has become increasingly difficult, due to a combination of increased public scrutiny, expectations of conduct and the ubiquity of faster, more transparent and truly international communications media.

Many of the tools used by individuals and external groups to put pressure on organisations to change their behaviours are not new. Companies active in South Africa during the 1970s were at the receiving end of shareholder divestment, pamphleteering and boycotts in protest at apartheid. What is different today is the extent of shareholder activism, the increased media and political lobbying skills of pressure groups and the speed with which local campaigns against corporate bad behaviour can take centre stage internationally.

This is not just because of the increased reach and speed of the media. The Internet has also had a major impact, affording even isolated individuals the opportunity to not only reach a large audience via websites and e-mail but also, as even internet savvy companies such as Yahoo!, Microsoft and Amazon.com have found to their cost, the ability to inflict serious damage on an organisation. Cyber attacks can take a number of forms, including cyber squatting, suck sites, spoof sites, or, more seriously, hacking and paralysis of e-commerce sites through denial of service spamming attacks.

Simultaneously, corporate reputation management is made more difficult by a growing range of ethical problems and public concerns, from genetically modified organisms and global warming to the issues of equality, privacy and data protection. Stakeholder expectations of the role companies, particularly large multinationals, should play in building a better world have also expanded into social issues as 'personal' and diverse as health and the work life balance.

Globalisation also creates a difficult ethical environment for businesses, given that standards, expectations and business rules differ enormously across the world. Add to this heady mix unprecedented scrutiny from non-governmental organisations (NGOs), themselves under increased pressure to grow memberships and raise funds, and it is not difficult for even the most scrupulous organisation to find its hard-won reputation on the line – overnight. Witness Nike's battering by NGOs for failing to ensure their workers around the world were all adult and paid a living wage.

So what actions does an organisation need to take to prevent or minimise the impact of a slur on its reputation or battering from pressure groups or anti-corporate activists? First, identify the ethical principles that underpin the company and measure these against those that would be expected of you by your stakeholders. The next stage is to undertake a social and environmental audit to identify gaps between principles and behaviour and areas where you are vulnerable to potential problems.

The audit should include a review of the organisation's mission statement and values as well as defining stakeholders and your impact on them. Stakeholders would generally include employees, customers, shareholders, investors, local and national regulators, suppliers and their employees, employee families, NGOs and the communities local to the areas where products may be sourced, manufactured, sold, used or disposed of. A mini audit should be carried out annually thereafter to ensure that standards are being met and new activities – such as donations to political parties, suppliers and projects – are not compromising the company.

Practical guidance on audit processes and content can be accessed easily through public relations consultants and organisations such as Business in the Community. Areas covered should include business conduct, employment and HR policies, health and safety, community involvement, environmental impact, procurement policies and the impacts of key suppliers – there is little point in getting into trouble over someone else's behaviour. Benchmark against what other companies are doing in the area of corporate social responsibility to identify best practice and minimum requirements.

It is vitally important to engage stakeholders regularly – even in cases where they appear relentlessly hostile to your organisation. Dialogue is important to understanding – and understanding may not result in agreement but it could facilitate compromise or prevent inappropriately aggressive actions. Equally, established two-way communication mediums allow you to address rumours faster, ensure that people have accurate information and highlight potential problems early. The most effective communications with 'critics' take place face to face in planned sessions and with individuals or small groups made up of representative individuals from different organisations. They also take place under a banner or setting that makes it clear you value their opinions and, if practicable, will accommodate them. Large public meetings are almost invariably a disaster.

Effective face-to-face dialogue can take a number of forms, from one-to-one issues-based meetings to stakeholder advisory panels that meet with the company on a regular basis to discuss its plans and place in the wider community. BT, Shell and Dow Chemicals are among a growing number of organisations that have put in place advisory panels of stakeholder representatives to give them better insight into perceptions and concerns.

The organisation's ethics policy should also be shared through mediums such as staff contracts, company publications and the website. It is important that the policy is realistic and represents the way that the organisation really does act and 'feel' – otherwise it will backfire and the company will appear hypocritical. The primary responsibility of a business is to increase shareholder value through profits, but within this constraint, the ethical principles should embrace the social or environmental goals important to stakeholders. Ensure that someone at director level, usually the lead for PR, understands that they are responsible for monitoring changes in the political, economic and social environment that may demand reviews of key elements of the ethics policy.

Anticipate that detractors are likely to purchase shares in order to gain access to meetings and apply pressure from within. This is an increasingly commonplace tactic. Greenpeace, for example, bought shares in BP Amoco in order to put forward a resolution in April 2000 urging the company to increase investment in solar energy and abandon plans to extract oil in the Arctic national Wildlife Refuge in Alaska. Do not try to eject such groups from AGMs or shareholder meetings but rather involve them in a wider shareholder engagement strategy.

A shareholder engagement programme is almost always of benefit. First, it gives you forums where a presentation of the facts and impacts of choices made can be presented proactively – which sometimes has the effect of turning idealists into realists and realists into company champions. Second, shareholder engagement can also steer you away from behaviours that may damage your reputation. Third, it increases your attractiveness to the growing number of socially concerned investors. Fourth, reputation impacts upon balance sheets and share prices. While conversations between companies and shareholders are still often a response to a specific resolution, they are increasingly broadening to embrace shareholder concerns not related to a planned or already filed resolution, or to allow the company to share company plans and strategies.

The annual report has traditionally served as the primary means by which companies communicate with shareholders on corporate financial performance. It can also provide an opportunity to include information relating to performance and activities on a variety of corporate social responsibility topics. The AGM is another opportunity to communicate with shareholders through a business presentation and question and answer sessions.

Forewarned is forearmed and, all too often, PRs are called in to lock the stable door long after the horse has bolted. Organisations vulnerable to pressure groups should ensure they monitor public opinion, gather intelligence and monitor the Internet message boards and websites of detractors. This may allow you to substitute rumours with facts before people become confrontational and set in their opposition. Even if your organisation is in the right, it is easy for a journalist or pressure group to make you look bad if when 'confronted' you do not have the full defending facts and independent expert support at your fingertips. CEOs will look even worse if they are caught out in a press interview by an example of corporate bad behaviour that they don't even know about. While you are busy marshalling facts and evidence, the pressure group is enjoying the full attention of the audience and setting the agenda – Brent Spar, for example, would have gone very differently if Shell's very credible defence had been communicated ahead of or alongside Greenpeace's apparently ill-informed attack.

Understand that you will never please everybody, and whilst you may turn idealists into realists through informed debate you are unlikely to move the truly radical. As there are people who are truly radical, you may be faced with battles that no one can win. Where possible, keep the battles short, and fight them with calm, rational facts rather than Goliath tactics. Aggressive legal threats, front groups and overt discrediting of individuals tend to backfire. McDonald's court action against the McLibel Two lost them more than it gained, attracting derision and attention to the claims of the two protesters around the world.

Conversely, cyber squatting is best dealt with by law if the offenders fail to respond to a gentle approach. Companies can get injunctions against blatant cases of cyber squatting and trademark infringement. There are also legal remedies to other aspects of cyber terrorism but the best form of defence is to ensure good fire-walls, properly set up filtering technology and proper user terms and conditions.

Don't forget the value of fast communications mechanisms for conveying facts and nailing rumours in times of crisis. E-mails and telephone calls should be used without hesitation for contacting people for whom a rumour may cause grave concern or other groups who may rush to give an ill-educated sound bite to the media – so fanning the flames and lending credence to disin-formation. A study by Oxford Executive Research into the impact of man-made catastrophes on the share value of multinational corporations found that those who recovered were those who gave rapid, credible responses. Important to recovery, particularly if the catastrophe was an accident resulting in loss of human life, was a CEO who responded quickly and acknowledged responsibility.

Last but not least, if you value your reputation, don't lie, don't cheat, don't bribe and don't steal. The benefits go way beyond escaping the attentions of pressure groups; evidence suggests that good corporate citizens hold onto skilled staff longer, perform better financially over time, loyal suppliers provide better value and consumer purchasing behaviour is affected by perceptions of an organisation. Furthermore, bad behaviour not only provokes public ire, it can also result in legislation, which is generally significantly more onerous than self-regulation and restraint.

Sara Render is Chief Executive of UK marcomms consultancy Kinross & Render Ltd., and a Director of ECCO, one of the world's 25 largest international PR networks.

Communities & mutual gains

Conventional PR can backfire with communities and interest groups, putting corporate reputations under severe pressure. There is a more productive way of managing contentious issues, say Dr Tom Watson and Steve Osborne-Brown.

Corporate reputations are often in greatest danger when the stakeholders are ignored, especially the communities in which corporations operate. The focus on financial and share performance blinds profit-led organisations to the contentious issues that surround their operations. Equally, all levels of government can be so driven by policy performance that they also lose sight of the people they serve.

James Grunig has identified four models of public relations practice – 'press agentry' and 'information dissemination' that he calls One-Way (outward only) and 'asymmetric' and 'symmetric' that he calls Two-Way. Without discussing the detail of Grunig's models, much of the persuasional public relations undertaken for large organisations is from the One-Way paradigm. This is the 'let's tell the people' approach using news releases to disseminate information.

While this may help raise awareness, it does not involve large organisations in a dialogue with their stakeholders and so they miss the feedback, the expressions of concern and the fear that their actions cause, especially in relation to land use and environmental plans.

Whatever side of the fence we sit on, there is almost an inevitability of disputes arising from land use issues. A lot of time is spent trying to reach agreement with others but, despite a co-operative spirit and every good intention, there are frequent frustrations. Time and money is wasted, credibility and reputations are lost, as appeals, public inquiries and litigation delay the ultimate – and, to some, incomprehensible – decision.

There is an obvious need for a radical change in procedures, attitudes and techniques if we are to end this vicious circle of claim and counter-claim, accusation, rebuttal and defence and go forward to reach an acceptable solution to disputes involving land use. It must move from One-Way to Two-Way public relations and negotiation.

A new and, some say, radical approach to dispute resolution has been developed in the USA at MIT/Harvard. Called Mutual Gains, this approach seeks to involve all parties in the decision-making process at the outset, giving a sense of ownership to every side and culminating in a 'win, win, win' solution. This approach has been tried and tested on many disputes in the States and, suitably adapted to the British mindset, could work equally well this side of the pond.

The author of the Mutual Gains approach, Professor Lawrence Susskind of the MIT/Harvard Public Disputes Program, published his Facility Siting Credo, containing guidelines for an effective land use decision process a decade ago. This, the forerunner of the Mutual Gains approach, has proved extremely successful in many, and varied, land use disputes in the US.

The Credo addressed the problems encountered in proposals to site facilities that, while generally viewed as being beneficial, were perceived by the potential host community to be noxious. Prisons, hospices, waste treatment plants, landfills, sewage treatment plants and, importantly, low-cost or social housing were all viewed as LULUs – Locally Unwanted Land Uses – in the eyes of the local communities.

The Credo sets a number of objectives to be met in the planning and development of LULUs and cites considerable success throughout the USA and Canada. Hallmark Public Relations adapted these principles to the British way of life and, launched as PR Negotiation, has since enjoyed considerable success utilising this methodology in the UK. It has been used in retail, industrial, leisure, educational and residential land situations.

The traditional methods employed by many corporations, developers and local authorities are perceived as a 'Decide, Dictate, Defend' approach in which only lip service is given to consultation and opponents are talked 'to' rather than 'with'. This only serves to fuel the very real anger felt by the community and other interest groups. Often it leads to letters, petitions and demonstrations. Minority groups form coalitions and committees, open websites and organise themselves into effective, well-led opposition groups. As a result, corporate reputations are under severe pressure.

The new approach, which promotes a much more effective 'Display, Discuss, Decide' process, addresses the real fears, concerns and anger felt by the affected community. Anger is a very powerful emotion that needs to be fully understood if progress is to be made. It can be attributed to any combination of four factors:

■ the reality – 'My way of life has been affected as a result of your actions';
■ the perception – 'Your proposals will affect my way of life';
■ the ideology – 'Your actions are morally/ethically wrong';
■ the impotency – 'You are picking on me'.

Simply telling people that you are right and they are wrong will only inflame the situation and further fuel their anger. A patronising 'It isn't/wasn't/won't be that bad really' only confirms their worst fears. Very often the opposition groups will genuinely not understand why an organisation has such a different view on matters. They either do not believe the benefits outweigh the risks or think that there are no benefits to them at all. Very often we are equally ignorant of their views. In this situation, hostility is inevitable.

Classic outward-only PR and communication methods are seen as obstructive and act to increase anger rather than control or dissipate it. These methods try to prove that 'the public' has not been adversely affected by something that has been done, play down the differences in values or attempt to prove that what you are trying to do is not risky or harmful.

So how can we avoid arousing such anger? What can we do to change perceptions and shape reality to make our proposals more acceptable? The Mutual Gains approach is founded on six basic principles that, if used with belief, can overcome the communications problems.

These are:

■ acknowledge the concerns of the other sides;
■ encourage joint fact finding;
■ offer contingent commitments to minimise impacts if they do occur;
■ accept responsibility – admit mistakes and share power;
■ act in a trustworthy fashion at all times;
■ focus on building long-term relationships.

It is important to consider more fully these six points and how we can implement them:

■ **Acknowledge concerns** – speak to them in a way that shows you understand; show empathy. Use this as a starting point for further discussion and recognise that they have as much right to their opinions as you do to yours.

■ **Joint fact-finding** – assume different interpretations of the same issues. Share information to avoid the battle of the printout and agree on the generation of information – research, reports, evaluation and monitoring.

■ **Contingent commitments** – offer compensation for unintentional (but knowable) effects.

■ **Accept responsibility** – worry about credibility and legitimacy. Without these virtues the other sides will believe there is no smoke without fire.

■ **Act in a trustworthy fashion** – transparency from the outset will strengthen trust in your organisation. If your counsel in the past has been to admit nothing and deny everything, ask yourself what this has actually achieved. Any sense that the other sides have been manipulated, trivialised, ignored or made to look like fools will fuel their anger and make a negotiated settlement extremely remote.

■ **Build long-term relationships** – we should all think long-term, particularly with sustainability being such a strong issue, and therefore need to build and maintain long-term relationships. Once again this will help build a credible reputation and assist in future proposals. If you care about your reputation you must work with all groups and individuals with an interest.

But how can these principles be put into action?

1. **Take the initiative:**
■ don't delay until you are put on the defensive;
■ try to shape perceptions of the problem and invent possible solutions;
■ minimise the extent to which others dictate your moves – be proactive rather than reactive.

2. **Seek consensus:**
■ design options to satisfy interests;
■ listen carefully to understand the interests of all stakeholders;
■ share responsibility for collecting data and finding solutions;
■ use neutral intermediaries or facilitators when appropriate.

3. **Emphasise outcomes:**

■ focus on solutions, not analyses;

■ be prepared to sacrifice comprehensiveness for relevance;

■ work backwards from goals and constraints (even though these will be revised);

■ link actions to outcomes.

4. **Enhance legitimacy:**

■ be trustworthy and truthful in all dealings;

■ strive for consistency;

■ minimise secrecy.

5. **Maintain credibility:**

■ always consult fully before making any decisions;

■ make realistic commitments, and…

■ …once again, minimise secrecy.

You will have noticed a strong common theme – transparency and openness. Large corporates and local government, in particular, are often accused of dictating to stakeholders and being covert in their methods. In many cases this is a perception rather than a reality. Unfortunately, to most people what they perceive is reality. Therefore we have to react to them in exactly the same way.

Public relations practice should not be megaphone diplomacy. To be effective in supporting and developing corporate reputations, it should be seeking mutual gains whenever possible. Not only will the corporate reputation improve, but also the reputation and perceived value of public relations.

Dr Tom Watson FIPR is Chairman of the Public Relations Consultants Association and Managing Director of Hallmark Public Relations. Steve Osborne-Brown MIPR is Account Director with Hallmark Public Relations. He heads the consultancy's PR Negotiation practice advising clients on planning issues and has attended the MIT-Harvard Public Disputes Program in Cambridge, Mass.

Public policy and regulators

Building a first-class reputation with political and official organisations strongly reinforces corporate reputation, complementing the traditional avenues of raising brand awareness, says Simon Nayyar, Executive Director of Citigate Public Affairs.

What's in a reputation? Well, potentially, quite a lot when it is at the mercy of politicians, civil servants and regulators.

FTSE 100 and mid 250 listed companies are increasingly recognising that building and sustaining a first-class corporate reputation with political and official audiences is as beneficial and necessary as establishing professional relationships with investors and the media. Excellent relations with public affairs audiences, which take a number of different guises, contribute to the virtuous circle of contented customers, staff and shareholders for any successful business.

Over the last 20 or so years, there has been a transformation in the amount of time and resources which companies have invested in their public affairs strategies in order to establish and maintain a good corporate reputation. The polished strategies of US-based companies have been increasingly adopted in the UK and are also being incorporated into European business practice. Greater resources are now earmarked for the development and execution of public affairs programmes, and organisations from the public and private sector are increasingly engaging professional public affairs consultancies to help them promote awareness, among political and official audiences, of themselves and their commercial issues.

It is, of course, not just quoted companies that need to sustain their reputation through paying due attention to the field of public affairs. Over the last ten years, the voluntary sector has also come to recognise the benefits of engaging with public affairs audiences, and as a result, their approaches to politicians have taken on an increasing sense of professionalism.

Public affairs audiences are, by political perspective, policy interest and geographical spread, diverse, although perhaps the most obvious sector for focus is that of the elected politicians. Backbench MPs – and, partly because of the pressure which back-benchers exert upon them, ministers – attach an enormous amount of sensitivity to business decision-making, with employment issues for constituents a particular area which affects corporate reputations in the political world. For example, if a supermarket chain or high street bank seeks to rationalise the number of branches it operates in any given area, it can expect that local politicians will attach a considerable amount of sensitivity to the process. During the run up to a general election, corporate reputation management in public affairs takes on even more significance, as consumers equal voters.

Away from the House of Commons, it is vital that attention is paid to political opinion formers other than MPs. Peers have a crucial – albeit largely misunderstood and unsung – role to play in the drafting of legislation in the UK, and have the opportunity to

express powerful opinions on public policy issues of direct consequence to all companies. Regionality must also be fully and
continuously taken into account, given the respective powers of
the Scottish Parliament and the Welsh and Northern Ireland
Assemblies, and the establishment of Regional Development
Agencies throughout England.

Aside from regional devolution in the UK, the European
agenda brings its own challenges, with companies having to
engage both the elected representatives of the European Parliament
and officials of relevant Directorates General within the European
Commission, each with their own distinct agenda. In addition,
corporate reputation management needs to take full account of
industry regulators and trade and professional associations.

Strategies for the establishment of a particular organisation as
a market leader and authoritative voice in its particular area of
business can be devised for each discrete political and official
audience. Each is informed by the nature of the company or body
and its commercial or organisational objectives. It is axiomatic
that a voluntary organisation aiming to raise its profile in order to
gain more government funding would approach its audience in a
different way from a company wishing to raise awareness among
consumers of a new market product or institutional investors
about the maximisation of shareholder value.

In any circumstance, a company or organisation would need to
have a thorough understanding of legislative and regulatory
activity in its sector in order to be successful in managing its
corporate reputation, so that the audience could be targeted and
informed in a professional way. Defining a communications
strategy which ensures that public affairs audiences understand
particular concerns is of increasing value to high profile
companies, as it allows them to make a significant contribution to
the development of public policy.

Recent political history has been characterised by efforts to
make legislative bodies more transparent in providing information
to key stakeholders. For the majority of organisations, however, it
is perhaps equally as important to contribute to the work of demo-

cratic institutions, thus ensuring that they can make the most effective contribution to the development of public policy. Such relationships offer the opportunity for companies to strongly reinforce their reputation, complementing the traditional avenues of raising brand awareness by concentrating on those key political audiences who have the power to make a practical difference to commercial environments and practices.

Politics can seriously damage your bottom line – ignore it at your peril.

Simon Nayyar is an Executive Director of Citigate Public Affairs and a specialist in mergers and acquisitions work and competition policy. Simon is also a member of the Board of Management of the Public Relations Consultants Association (PRCA), and is Chairman of the PRCA's Public Affairs Committee. Citigate Public Affairs is one of the UK's premier public affairs consultancies. Based in Westminster, it also has offices in Edinburgh, Cardiff and Brussels. Citigate Public Affairs is a member of both the PRCA and the Association of Professional Political Consultants (APPC).

Investor relations

Investor relations are being 'consumerised', says Brian Basham of the Equity.i.Group. To achieve proper value, companies have to reach private investors directly and treat them like clients and customers.

Over the last ten years a major change has taken place in stock markets. This has been driven by an aggregation of investment funds into fewer and fewer hands. The trend has accelerated in recent years.

Pension funds are the largest constituent of the marketplace and in 1997, 37 of the large fund management companies controlled 85 per cent of all pension fund equities. In 1996, 26 such funds controlled 85 per cent of pension fund equities and last year it was down to 20. The rate of aggregation continues so that it is probable today that five of the largest fund management companies control some 50 per cent of all equities.

The effect on the stock market has been dramatic as these mega funds strive to increase the returns, not only to their clients (whose funds they manage) but also to their shareholders. In their drive to increase shareholder returns, the funds have done what any other business manager would do – they have attempted to achieve economies of scale by reducing overhead whilst maintaining margins and turnover.

As a consequence, the funds have been forced to follow fewer and fewer stocks and those they've chosen, quite naturally, are the very largest, in which they can deal in volume. One fund manager told me recently that when he started his business in 1974 he could 'go to 300 funds with £100 million to invest'. Those funds could afford to invest in relatively small tranches. Today the mega funds cannot afford that luxury. They need to invest huge sums in very large companies to be competitive against other managers for funds to invest.

As a consequence the share prices of the top 350 companies have been driven up by huge demand while those of the smaller companies have drifted downwards through lack of interest (and occasionally wholesale dumping of stock).

The consequence is a top-heavy distorted marketplace. Today, there are 1,886 companies quoted on the London Stock Exchange (excluding foreign register companies) marketplace with a market capitalisation between them of some £1.83 trillion. The top 350 account for £1.74 trillion – or 94 per cent of that value – and the bottom 1,500 or so account for just £107 billion. Vodafone on its own, at £166 billion, is larger than all these 1,500 companies together.

Stripping out the dotcoms, the whole of the smaller quoted company marketplace is quoted at just £80 billion and with an average price earnings ratio (p/e) of 15 against the 26 p/e of the top 350 companies.

This represents a huge challenge for the country as well as the smaller companies. The undervaluation of the smaller company market has direct impact on employment and growth – it's a fact of life that big companies tend to shed employees, small companies take them on. If, as many fear, the major companies are tremendously over-valued, that's very worrying indeed. As the population ages and fund management companies are forced to sell stock to meet their pension requirements, then these share prices could collapse.

The message for corporate managers of public companies and those wishing to go public is clear – in today's market the big investing institutions must be courted because they are far and away the biggest source of funds, but managers must also look elsewhere for support.

However, all is not lost. While the major institutions have been walking away from the market, private investors have been taking much more interest and, moreover, they have been helped by the development of IT services, particularly the web which has the capacity both to deliver information to them in a timely fashion and to enable them to invest in the market on the cheapest possible terms.

Whilst the institutions continue to 'own' the vast majority of equities, private investors are the most active traders in these companies. Of course, it is the daily trades which most go to affect the price of those companies.

The task for the vast majority of quoted companies therefore is a new one. They must maintain their relationship with the 'owners' of their shares, but they must now turn their attention to the new market which is represented by private investors and herein lies a paradox.

Companies which are experts at selling their goods and services find it difficult to transpose their culture through the finance director (sometimes the barrier) into marketing their stocks and shares. If under-rated companies are to achieve a proper rating for their equity, they need to learn the lesson quickly. The only way in which they are going to achieve proper value is to understand how they can best reach private investors and to treat them as they do their clients and customers. We call it 'the consumerisation of investor relations'.

Brian Basham is a well-known, leading financial public relations practitioner and successful entrepreneur. He is also a writer and contributes to financial journals and periodicals. He was a member of the CBI Wider Share Ownership Task Force. Recently he was instigator and Deputy Chairman of the Treasury SQC Group. He is a Director of Mezzanine Group plc. He is Founder and Chairman of the financial public relations business, Basham & Co., and of the Internet publishing business, InterShare. He is Founder and Deputy Chairman of Equity Development.

Organisational culture and change

Charged with translating activity into meaning, leaders and managers are only as good as their communication skills, says Colette Dorward of Smythe Dorward Lambert.

People exist through dialogue, say the theorists. The interactions between people, that we call conversations, cause us to understand ourselves and so become whole. The same can be said of organisations – we need to transact to survive. Now that corporate managers all understand the need to articulate and share their vision, their corporate policies and their unique selling proposition (USP) as an employer, as a service provider or as a maker of goods, what is impeding the abilities of organisations to orchestrate the conversations that will optimise success?

Maybe nothing more complicated than the race to keep up with a rapidly changing social dynamic that is causing those in the developed world who are employed (as opposed to those in less developed places that 'merely' work to exist) to reframe our relationship with what used to be called gainful employment.

The changing dynamic is most visible at the very fringes of the world of work, where ethical groups and anarchists, do-gooders and political extremists are taking to the streets in leaderless and unmanaged groups to voice protest against the heavy hand of global economic manipulation. Will Hutton, in a recent *Observer* article on the Danish referendum on joining the euro, summarises the threat:

> *The urgent need is to reconnect politics and people. European institutions are being built on sand unless and until they can co-exist with and foster the urgent requirement for identity, belonging and participation that globalisation is bringing in its train.*

Now we are seeing something of the same dynamic relationship between employees and the employed. The most common plea from my clients is how do we go about increasing our people's sense of 'connected-ness' – or even how do we manufacture it from a standing start? And it's not just all about speed. Speed of change is, of course, the most extraordinary and consistent feature of life at work today – from technological and genetic breakthroughs to revolving door CEOs – but it's the type of underlying change that is important. The seismic shift in personal choice.

Lets look at three different drivers behind the question of 'connected-ness', and some possible responses.

Personalisation: for some its an obscenity, for some a right. Stand in the queue at any Starbucks outlet and listen to the confident litany of options that people exercise over how their coffee/milk/water combo should be presented. The corollary at work is a need – nay, an expectation – to be treated as an individual and to be able to influence the way work is done. In driving the shift from communication push to communication pull, the individual expects all the information ingredients to be available and also to assemble these – in terms of time, place and interactivity – in a way that suits them.

A stable point in a turning world: for some organisations this can be a double-edged sword. People need to understand and identify with an organisation's corporate values, it is argued, to provide meaning, purpose and personal alignment. A great deal of current work on changing culture centres on the clear articulation of corporate values and the provision of ways for people to experience these for themselves and respond to them. But with publication go transparency and accountability – and those most cringe-making features of corporate life, whether conveyed on laminated cards or large scale theatrics, attempts to reduce the style and standards of the organisation to behavioural dictats. The corporate harbour is filling up with the rusting hulks of legacy businesses that have failed to inject enough dynamism into their stable successful worlds. No doubt there are more to follow that will founder on an arrogant assumption about the relevance of what they are saying or doing to their people or their marketplaces.

Power shift in the skill base: this is a technology-driven phenomenon that is not new but is massively accelerating. Its not just that some jobs are disappearing due to today's version of automation, or that the primacy of front line staff – the inverted triangle of organisational structure – is, at last, endemic, but that the roles of those who manage and lead others is now under intensive and relentless scrutiny. The vulnerable members of the work society are not those with technical skills (provided they are able to keep abreast of changes) but those charged with translating activity into meaning. Living by their wits and their relationships, leaders and managers are only as good as their communication skills. The invasive nature of today's media – particularly electronic – means there is little room or time to hide before mistakes or indelicacies become public property.

Having passed through the phase of corporate control (top-down communication strategies, company knows best), to the phase of empowerment (driving shared standards and values through more participative and involving employment environments), organisations are now occupying the role of host. The host may own a brand and nurture stakeholders' experience of that brand (even though they may 'own' very few, if any, of the people who influence that experience). But as employees we look to them as enablers or facilitators of our work experience, as temporary purchasers of our skills and, to some extent, our time.

The seismic shift in personal choice puts communication – and particularly the dialogue between host and worker – at a premium. Our role as communicators is to facilitate and enable that dialogue.

Colette Dorward is a partner at Smythe Dorward Lambert.

Employee expectations

Employee Communications is about more than winning the war for talent. It is about encouraging people to safeguard and champion your reputation, says Tari Hibbitt

Internal communications is now recognised as more than just about retaining people. It is about ensuring that your workforce contributes, in a positive way, to the company's reputation. To do this, they need to understand where the business is going and that they support and carry through the company's vision, mission and values. To be fully effective, it must be part of the whole senior management teams' responsibility. However, this is the area where good intentions frequently break down.

Today's employees expect to be much more engaged with their employer. They expect to be consulted in the setting of their own and their department's goals, and they need to know how their contribution is linked to the company's success. There should be a clear link between individual, division or team, and overall corporate goals of the organisation. Effectively communicating these goals, becomes a critical part of motivating the workforce.

In an increasingly competitive market place where it is more and more difficult to differentiate between products or services, it is very often 'our people' who give a company that point of difference that differentiates its brand from all its competitors.

Staff are more likely to feel motivated and loyal if they are kept informed about progress. Successful employee engagement programmes are rooted in the premise that healthy organisational relationships are based on trust, respect and commitment. Research has shown that employee satisfaction has a direct correlation with customer satisfaction, which in turn directly impacts on financial results.

In any company staff will leave, but they should be leaving for a better job, not for a better company. And how important it is, that staff who are moving on, leave with positive feelings about their time in the company. Conducting exit interviews, and acting on the information gained, is a vital in creating a positive working environment for the future.

Attracting talent

Today it is the employees who hold the balance of power when it comes to deciding where to work. The reputation of the company will be a vital component in the decision-making process. No one wants their friends or colleagues to say 'You're going to work for who?', when they announce their new job.

Candidates routinely use the web to find out about companies before their first interview and the company's own web site will project a positive image. But chat rooms and associated sites may hold less than flattering views about the company. Disillusioned employees, pressure groups or other activists may have an axe to grind on employee relations, environmental concerns or the use of child labour.

To find out what sort of employer a company really is, a wise interview candidate will ensure they meet as many of their potential work colleagues as possible at interview stage. Can every company truly say that this would be a positive experience for a prospective employee?

Developing talent

Today's workforce also has expectations about their own careers and future development. Few people are content to stand still. The employer who sets clear goals for individuals and identifies training needs to help them achieve their potential, will benefit from a well motivated team. The provision of a progressive and comprehensive training programme will often be the deciding factor in choosing a job, and considerably aids retention.

But running training courses is not enough in itself. They must be relevant, tailored to the needs of the individual and clearly communicated in terms of the objectives they are to achieve. Once completed, there must be a system in place for evaluating the success of the training and identifying, with the individual and their line manager, how the training is helping them to achieve their goals, and how they can progress.

Idea generation

In the new economy, managers realise that good ideas are just as likely to come from junior staff as they are from senior, or administrative staff rather than marketing and business managers.

This changes the nature of leadership. Leaders used to hold the power and communicate down to the workers, telling them what to do. Today's successful leaders have to have the vision, but they also have to ask their workers, 'What do you need from me? What can I provide for you that you can't provide for yourselves?' This is true empowerment, where workers' views and ideas are valued and leaders provide support as well as direction.

A new employee with a fresh perspective may be the person who comes up with something that will revolutionise the way you do business. However, you will never find out unless you create an environment where people know it's OK to make suggestions and contribute. In this communicative age, staff meetings or team meetings are a more appropriate place to encourage staff to contribute than the traditional 'suggestion box'.

The company networks

The formal ways in which internal communications operates in a company may have changed, but the informal ways still exist in much the same way as they always have. Gossip, whether in the loos, at the coffee machine or in the staff canteen will always be a potent channel for passing on information, both good and bad. But the most potent new channel is, of course, e-mail and the Internet or Intranet.

Companies should allow employees to use these methods to exchange news and views, unless the content of messages is illegal or likely to lead to litigation. People use the Internet and e-mail like they used to use the telephone, and as long as employees are delivering against their goals and staff morale is good, there should not be a need to police the use of these channels. If a company feels the need to control their use, then there is a problem.

Techniques

Newsletters, company news, messages from the CEO or information on what the media is saying about the company, can all be communicated quicker and more effectively using electronic rather than printed means.

On-line chats work well too, using conference calls or if available, video conferencing, to unite workers at a number of sites across one or more countries or continents.

But it is easy to be bedazzled by 'whiz bang' technologically advanced solutions and forget that face-to-face communication is still the best method of communication for many types of information, particularly where emotions or relationships are involved. The web excels at providing fast communication, particularly to a multi-site workforce, but careful thought must be given as to how and when it is used.

It may be appropriate to use e-mail for fast communication to senior managers, but then brief them to cascade the information down to the rest of the work-force through a series of internal staff meetings. Fast, open and honest communication will only be successful if you deal with the bad news in the same way as the good. Staff will not trust an organisation that hypes up all the good news and tries to sweep the bad news under the carpet.

Be honest about the bad news, allow the staff to grieve and voice their concerns and then be positive about what you are doing to take the business forward. The challenge is to manage the communication and beat the grapevine.

When celebrating success, be spontaneous and join in the process. E-mail is a brilliant tool, but also incredibly dangerous. The speed, brevity and informality of e-mail communication can often turn an innocuous message into a potential conflict situation. It should never be used to deal with personal conflict. Pick up the phone or walk to the person's desk Never allow a slanging match to develop on e-mail.

In adversity

There is nothing worse than employees finding out what is going on from the media, just because the media were more demanding. For this reason, any crisis plan must have a section on employee communications.

In a takeover, there may be legal complications, governing the disclosure of information. There is a particular danger of employees being left in the dark, which can be compounded if different time zones are involved. It is difficult to abide by stock market regulations in New York and do the right thing by employees in Spain. Consider an e-mail blast, a voice mail blast or an all staff meeting. Or all three. And remember that stock exchange rules may say that no one can know before investors, but newswires take minutes, so there is time to communicate with employees.

Openness should also apply to relations with unions. Their role has changed dramatically in recent years, and they have to be involved from early on. They are your supporters, not your enemies.

Measures

How is the success of your employee communications measured? Staff turnover, trends in productivity and ease of recruitment are obvious ways. The other way is to check morale, either through employee questionnaires or focus groups. Some form of regular employee satisfaction measure should be on every company's agenda. 360§ appraisals are a valuable tool in assessing how staff view their managers, and can cover issues such as internal communications. Asking customers and clients how they feel about your company is another useful method, customers have an unhealthy knack of picking up on disquiet.

If your organisation is leaking like a sieve, you can be pretty sure you've got a problem. You should be able to pass on confidentialities to trusted colleagues and know they will be treated as such.

It is vital to keep some form of measure running on a continuous basis. Managers broadly understand the theory of employee communications, but many organisations still just pay lip service to it. A one-off staff survey, with no feedback of results and no action as a result, will do more harm than good and just encourage cynicism about the company's motives.

Your employees should truly be the champions of your company's reputation.

Tari Hibbitt is Chief Executive of Edelman PR Worldwide's London office. Founded in 1952, Edelman PR Worldwide is the world's fifth largest public relations consultancy with annual fees of £200million. It has 41 offices around the world employing 2000 professional staff.

3

Responses

Unified communications structures

Shell has learnt to manage its reputation in a way that strikes a balance between global and local. John Williams of Fishburn Hedges gives an insider's view to how it restored its 'licence to operate'.

One of the biggest challenges in corporate reputation management is the management itself. It is increasingly difficult for multinational companies to balance global and local needs.

This is in part due to some contradictory trends. Your reputation has to be managed globally – we live in what Shell calls a 'CNN World': television pictures can be beamed instantly around the world, even from war zones and protest marches. The World Wide Web allows instant sharing of news and opinions, and calls to action. Issues are becoming increasingly global – from world trade rules to tackling global warming. Your actions in one part of the world cannot be shielded from observation and impact in other countries and other markets.

Yet for the most part, the people of the planet who hold and shape corporate reputation are resolutely local, even those who spend most of their time on planes. They all have a first language. They are nearly all rooted in the culture of the country or region in which they grew up. They are likely to turn first to local media for their window on the world. They have different and diverse values systems. It is impossible to talk to them all through one medium and with one message.

Multinationals share those characteristics, which makes them so hard to manage. The balance of global and local is hard to strike. Command and control structures can create uniformity but are inflexible and slow. Devolved structures can be inconsistent and unpredictable. Most companies end up somewhere in the middle. All this impacts on reputation management: many of the most high profile failures of corporate reputation have been created or severely exacerbated by management failure; head offices being out of touch with opinion in local markets, or unable to assess the importance of local problems; a system slow to react to incidents, or to share information across borders; an inability to apply corporate rules and policies consistently across the globe, or simply breathtaking head office arrogance that what goes for the home market will be right for the rest of the world.

Shell was aware of all these issues when it planned its first active global corporate reputation programme, which was launched in March 1999. Shell's strategy offers some lessons for a unified approach.

Shell's approach

Shell's programme has its origins in the twin attacks it faced in 1995, when its reputation, principles and practices were so widely challenged over the issues of human rights in Nigeria surrounding the execution of Ken Sawo-Wiwa, and the plans to dispose of the Brent Spar oil storage platform in the North Sea. The criticisms Shell faced shocked the organisation, which prided itself on a long tradition of social responsibility. It realised it was out of touch with public opinion and needed to respond, to protect and restore its 'licence to operate'.

The first step was to conduct a comprehensive exercise to get a picture of world opinion of the Group. The programme was called 'Society's Changing Expectations' and involved detailed market research among employees, the general public, special publics (Shell's term for opinion-leaders) and senior managers across more than 25 countries, as well as a series of stakeholder round table discussions and peer group benchmarking.

The research helped Shell identify what it called a 'knowledge gap' – a lack of understanding of Shell's values and approach, with specific concern over issues of environmental responsibility and human rights.

The global scale of this research and analysis gave real weight and momentum to implementing solutions. Shell had to start with its policies and practices: reviewing and strengthening its Statement of General Business Principles to include a specific commitment to sustainable development; creating policies on climate change aiming to match and exceed the Kyoto protocol targets; and committing to greater accountability through publishing the Shell Report, a report to society covering all areas of company performance: financial, environmental and social.

However, good practice was not enough. Shell recognised it needed a programme to manage its reputation actively, to engage stakeholders and to communicate with them.

The programme was run internally by a small reputation support team within Shell International, reporting initially to External Affairs, but later transferred to the Sustainable Development team to emphasise the link between implementing and reporting on Shell's commitment to sustainable development, and its wider reputation management programme.

The approach was supervised by a steering committee, initially headed by Sir Mark Moody-Stuart, the Chairman of the Committee of Managing Directors. The lead of Shell's most senior executive emphasised the commitment to the programme from the top – an important and unifying internal signal. The steering committee included senior representatives of Shell's business divisions, major country operations as well as key head office functions including marketing and HR. This was crucial to achieve collective support and responsibility for the campaign, especially from the five Global Businesses.

The agency selection was unusual. Shell felt that special publics needed a greater degree of personal communication and engagement to complement the more traditional mass medium of corporate advertising. Shell called this a PR-led approach. It recognised that advertising alone was, though powerful, too blunt a medium to achieve Shell's objectives. What was needed was a programme that could take a variety of messages to a range of audience groups through a spread of different media.

Thus the PR agency Fishburn Hedges was appointed as 'lead agency' to work alongside J Walter Thompson to develop a joint strategy and a range of communication tools and vehicles. The client and agency team has worked closely together, alongside research, media buying, web advertising and database management agencies. This core team, which has worked together for over two years, often meeting weekly, has been crucial to keeping a consistency of message and execution.

The strategy itself recognised that the reputation programme would only ever be a fraction of Shell's total communications with the outside from marketing campaigns to investor relations. Therefore it was invaluable to devise a reputation management framework which demonstrated how the reputation campaign fitted in with other corporate communications, particularly about the business transformation that the group was driving to improve its return on capital and its investor rating. This allowed others to see the core campaign theme of Shell's commitment to sustainable development as complementary and not conflicting with other messages, programmes and strategies delivered by the Businesses or local operations.

Another crucial part of unified thinking was to recognise the global reach of special publics, but also to acknowledge their diversity and different perspectives. Thus the main audience for the campaign was to be global special publics but segmented and tracked in six different global groups: the investment community; non-governmental organisations (NGOs) and intergovernmental organisations (IGOs); the media; government and politicians; peers in other major corporations; and academics and gurus (business pundits and advisers).

The real challenge of the campaign has been in implementing the programme, where local delivery is crucial. The central idea has been to stimulate debate about the issues underlying sustainable development, to set out Shell's approach but invite discussion and debate on the need to balance 'profits and principles'. Advertising itself became a PR tool, through a centrally planned campaign in global media. This was integrated with links to a dedicated part of the shell.com website, which allowed feedback and debate. The advertising and website created a global footprint for each local country to support, and a toolkit was created to encourage engagement with local special publics by each country operation. These included a full press pack, two booklets describing the campaign approach and core elements for internal and external distribution, employee briefing packs, a template to conduct local stakeholder forums and, from 2000, a short form version of the Shell sustainable development report, to allow easier translation and wider distribution.

The take-up of the local tools has been encouraged by annual regional workshops to brief local communications managers and to provide constant support and communication by e-mail through the year. Further ideas, including a writing prize run with *The Economist*, have been added to the toolkit. The take-up has been good: well over half of Shell's country operations have used the material, with 20 of the bigger countries adopting the advertising for local use. Tracking research among global special publics (those with an international influence) has been conducted and there has been a positive shift in attitudes. Most strikingly, hits on the shell.com website rose from under 4 million a month before the programme started to over 9 million in the first few months, a level that has been maintained since.

John Williams is an independent consultant and non-executive director of Fishburn Hedges, a company he co-founded. He has specialised in reputation management and corporate branding and his clients at Fishburn Hedges have included Shell International, PricewaterhouseCoopers and McDonald's.

Fishburn Hedges is one of the UK's leading corporate communications companies, with a focus on PR, public affairs, internal communication and design. Clients range from BT and Unilever to PowerGen, Abbey National and the DETR. It was one of the first companies to set up a corporate ethics and social responsibility practice and its clients include several not-for-profit organisations.

Recruiting & rewarding professionals

Wall Street has caught onto PR as a growth story, says Harris Diamond, President and Chief Executive of BSMG Worldwide, but if the industry is to retain its position as the cream of the crop in the marketing spectrum, then it must find ways to attract and retain the best talent.

Developments in the information age economy are opening up unprecedented opportunities for people who work in the PR industry. But those same developments create new challenges and threats that affect our most important asset – our people.

The PR industry is going through a period of unprecedented growth and today we have a new industry paradigm: media channels are fragmenting, news and entertainment are converging and the Internet is creating both opportunities and threats. We are seeing more emphasis on the importance of branding, the role of internal communications and investor relations, and growing integration across marketing services. Much of this is being brought about by a new wave of CEOs who are changing the way business operates and presenting advisers from the communications industry and other professional services with new challenges.

The growth of PR has not escaped the attention of Wall Street. Analysts recognise the potential of our industry and its non-cyclical nature. They have recognised the rapid consolidation among PR firms leading to the integration of services, the dramatic increase in fees and the fact that billings of $3 million to $5 million are not unusual. The financial market also recognises the inherent strength of PR in its ability to build deep and long-lasting relationships with the most senior levels of client management.

Importantly, Wall Street acknowledges the growth and profitability of PR vs advertising. It would be fair to say that the PR industry is about where the advertising industry was ten years ago – we are the cream of the crop in the marketing spectrum. You have only to look at the contribution that PR is making to the fortunes of the major communications groups to understand the significance of this.

The PR industry's growth rate of 20 per cent in 1988 was four times that of the advertising industry. But before we get too complacent, let's reflect on what has been happening in advertising to see what can be learned. Recession totally changed the dynamics of advertising. Most notably, ad agencies found themselves in a highly competitive environment in which they were forced to evolve from a commission structure to one of negotiated fees. They suffered from lower profits and started to lose some of their best people to client firms and other professional service industries.

To avoid the same erosion happening in PR and to maintain premium pricing, we have to focus on what we do best. Our key strength is our ability to understand and manage an integrated communications approach. We have to sustain, develop and promote our skills in media strategy and press relations, the contribution we can make to brand and product marketing, our understanding of community relations and grass roots issues, our command of research and the complementary role of advertising, our grasp of the dynamics of the Internet, and most importantly, our skills in counselling the CEO.

PR faces three major challenges. First, we have to keep our costs under control. Second, while understanding and managing the concept of integrated communications, we must differentiate PR from other professional advisers. Third, we have to retain the people who will help us sustain this golden age of PR. We must stop defection to the client side, and counter the attractions of higher rewards and broader opportunities that are being held out by other professions.

We hear about the growing convergence with other professional services industry providers such as management consultants and accountancy firms, and the risk that may invade our territory, raising issues for the PR industry of career choice, remuneration and loyalty. Personally, I don't feel threatened from that direction. They can't do what we do. They don't understand how to build reputation or enhance brand strengths. PR adds a unique value to what our clients do.

We should draw comfort from the fact that while the PR industry is still attracting people, a top management consultancy is reported to lose 17 per cent of its staff every year. While advertising fights to keep a presence in the CEOs office, PR counsellors are still in there.

So what do we have to do to sustain PR as the career of choice and to attract the best people? Well, for a start, we might consider making ourselves more attractive to the best talent in other professional service industries and dipping into the same talent pools as our clients – the consulting firms.

Public relations must provide leading-edge workplace benefits which not only include attractive compensation packages, training and professional development, and better technological services, but facilities that help people balance their personal and their professional lives.

We should provide facilities so that people can work effectively by telecommuting or through satellite offices. In an industry with a high female population, we need more childcare support, which can dramatically reduce staff turnover.

Our growth and profitability is linked to the quality of talent in our business. Continued success depends on our ability to work harder and faster than our competitors in recruiting, retaining and rewarding people.

Harris Diamond is President and Chief Executive officer of BSMG Worldwide, one of the largest and fastest-growing international communications firms.

A unit of True North Communications, BSMG Worldwide specialises in public relations, marketing communications, corporate communications, financial and transactional communications, public affairs, issues and advocacy advertising, and research and measurement. The firm has offices in 33 key cities and 15 countries around the globe, and affiliate relationships in an additional 40 countries.

Mr. Diamond also serves as Chairman of True North Diversified Companies, a division of True North Communications Inc. (NYSE: TNO), one of the world's leading advertising and communications holding companies. Based in Chicago, True North had 1999 revenues of approximately $1.4 billion and annual billings of more than $14 billion.

PR Week named Mr. Diamond 'PR Professional of the Year, 2000'. He was also named '1999 CEO All-Star' by Reputation Management magazine for his management of BSMG Worldwide, which noted that the firm has become, 'an example of the way communication can and should be integrated'. Regarded as one of the industry's leading experts in corporate and industry positioning, Mr. Diamond has counselled Fortune 500 companies undergoing profound change in environments of intense public scrutiny. While specialising in crisis and change management, he also provides ongoing strategic communications counsel to an array of clients, including several industry and trade associations.

Managing corporate reputation through crisis

If corporate activities are seen to be damaging, badly managed, secretive or insensitive, then an adverse event can easily escalate into a crisis. A more sophisticated and anticipatory approach is called for, says Mike Regester of Regester Larkin.

Crises that create the greatest public interest are those commonly described as 'disasters', such as aeroplane and rail crashes, involving tragic loss of life. The scrutiny of those perceived to be responsible for such events is intense, as seen recently with the Southall rail inquiry and the Paddington rail crash. The importance of demonstrating responsibility and accountability grows with each disaster.

Crises are not confined to disaster events, however. They come in as many varieties as the common cold. They can occur for reasons as diverse as safety lapses, litigation or unethical behaviour. The costs of a crisis can also be varied. Damage to reputation can have far-reaching implications beyond an initial financial loss. Product boycott; share price collapse; loss of competitive advantage; damaging legacy issues; and the imposition of restrictive regulation can be some of the more damaging consequences.

The definition of what constitutes a crisis is changing. Public perception of risk is frequently out of kilter with statistical evidence. Often, emotive and negative publicity becomes more important than an objective appraisal of risk probabilities. If corporate activities are regularly perceived to be damaging, badly managed, secretive or insensitive, as is often the case, this can turn an adverse event into a crisis situation. As a result of the growing importance of social responsibility and public accountability, there is a need for a much more sophisticated and anticipatory approach to safeguarding reputation.

There are two key points to bear in mind when considering crisis management. First, a crisis often does not suddenly manifest itself but can 'creep' up on a company over a long period of time. Developments which appear minor can reach crisis proportions. Therefore, issues of awareness and anticipation are key. These are often neglected, however, because of a short-term focus within many companies. Second, a company needs to demonstrate awareness of how it is perceived among key stakeholder groups. It

Is There a Gap?

PERFORMANCE — COMMUNICATION — PERCEPTION

Examine external perceptions
Accept them, justified or not
Close the gap

Understand that expectations will rise

Fig. 3.3.1: The gap between public perception of a company and its actual performance

needs to take on board that 'perception is the reality'. 'Outside-in' thinking – the ability of an organisation to view itself from the perspective of stakeholders – should be the key when companies engage in planning and decision-making.

The cost of catastrophe

In many cases, the damage to a company's reputation from a crisis only becomes apparent months or even years after the event. This is particularly true when an event is followed by investigations, government inquiries and legal action. Attempts to put a price on crisis, and its attendant reputational damage, is still an emerging area of expertise, but the following widely accepted estimates give an indication of how seriously crisis can affect the bottom line:

Exxon (Valdez spill)	$13 billion
Pan Am (Lockerbie crash)	$652 million
P&O (sinking at Zeebrugge)	$70 million
Union Carbide (Bhopal)	$527 million
Perrier (benzene incident)	$263 million
Occidental Oil (Piper Alpha)	$1,400 million
Barings Bank (collapse)	$900 million

These figures represent not only the cleanup costs and days of lost production but include product boycotts and recalls, falling markets and share prices, escalating compensation and brand reputational damage.

Consequences of a crisis

Failure to manage stakeholder perceptions in a crisis will lead to damage to reputation which always impacts the bottom line, in a combination of the following:

Product/service boycott or abandonment

Product-related crises alone range from outright failure, as in the case of the Carlsberg-Tetley widget (which resulted in the

withdrawal of millions of cans from the market), to the unantic-
ipated side effects of pharmaceutical products such as Ely
Lilly's drug, Opren, to treat arthritis symptoms (which caused
skin discoloration and sun intolerance in its users). Product
contamination, as experienced by Lucozade, Perrier and
Tylenol, are yet further examples.

Boycotts occur when stakeholders' initial shock at what has
happened escalates into anger because of a perceived lack of
concern, control or commitment. This anger is often fuelled by
media coverage and by the activity of advocacy groups. Following
the Pan Am crash at Lockerbie in 1988, anger mounted as the
company denied bomb warnings, failed to communicate with the
public or offer assistance to the bereaved. Hostility deepened
during the investigations which followed, and led to a sustained
passenger boycott. Pan Am went bankrupt in 1991.

Share price collapse

This occurs when institutional investors lose confidence in
management, not because of the crisis event but perceptions of
management's ability to deal with it. Weakened share price may
be temporary, but it may also result in a predator takeover bid, as
happened with French drinks company Perrier. When traces of
benzene were found in its bottled water, Perrier decided that
French consumers were less neurotic than their American counter-
parts and chose to dismiss it as 'a little affair which, in a few days,
will all be forgotten'. These remarks were reported in other key
markets, causing outrage about the company's lack of concern and
failure to implement a worldwide product recall. Perrier's share
price fell as it lost its status as market leader, and the company
became vulnerable to predators. Nestlé soon swallowed it up.

Loss of competitive advantage

The wider the gap between stakeholder expectations and a
company's performance, the easier it becomes for competitors to
take advantage of the opportunity to appeal to those expectations.

For example, Coca-Cola's flawed handling of a health scare in Belgium involving children led to a product ban by the Belgian government, which spread across much of Europe. When the ban was lifted, Coca-Cola had to take drastic measures, supplying free drinks to over a third of the Belgian and French populations, in an attempt to recover its share of the highly competitive European soft drinks market.

If a crisis is generalised across a product group, destroying stakeholder solidarity and confidence, it can ruin the entire market in favour of a different type of product. This happened in the fiasco surrounding the introduction of GM products in the UK. Monsanto were forced to conclude in 1999 that its mishandling of the issues had frustrated retailers' attempts to introduce and promote GM products and forced supermarkets to respond to customer concerns by withdrawing GM foods. This contributed to the rapid ruination of the market for GM products in Europe.

Damaging legacy issues

When a crisis damages the reputation of a company, the result is often to expose other aspects of its activities to scrutiny. The most prominent example of this in recent years is the sustained criticism of Railtrack, the UK train operator. Already perceived as profiteering and careless after the Southall crash and general passenger disgruntlement about poor services, Railtrack had no credit in the reputational bank when two trains crashed at Paddington in October 1999. The media immediately linked the Paddington crash to the earlier Southall accident. Railtrack's professed commitment to safety was ineffective because of the enduring perception of the company as neglectful of its stakeholders. The legacy of Paddington will continue to stalk the company's every move, from the activities of team away-days to each quarterly financial statement.

BP's international activities have been similarly dogged by the legacy of a scandal following a World in Action programme in 1997 on human rights violations and secret police training in its

Colombian operations. The company handled the accusations defensively, leading to entrenched opposition which has made it difficult to draw a line under the issue.

Imposition of new, restrictive regulation

The failure by one company to communicate effectively during a crisis can tarnish the reputation of an entire industry. Governments are prompted to 'be seen to police' the apparently errant behaviour of the sector concerned. Following the Exxon Valdez oil spill, for example, new regulations on double hulls for oil tankers were imposed on the entire industry by the US and UK governments. This regulatory change was not only costly, but it is widely believed by experts to weaken tanker structure and create new risks.

More recently, in 1998, a similar outcome followed the TWA 800 plane crash in Long Island, with the introduction of 'passenger rights' legislation.

Understanding and avoiding crisis creep

Analysis indicates that crises usually result from one or more of the following reputation risks:

- safety;
- service shortfall, often leading to service abandonment;
- unethical behaviour;
- public policy change;
- product/professional liability;
- major adverse event/publication;
- environmental damage;
- poor corporate governance;
- product recall/failure; and
- litigation.

Of course, not every possible crisis is foreseeable. However, research shows that corporate crises usually happen because of slow-burn 'crisis creep' risk issues which are allowed to become full-blown crises through poor strategic management. 'Crisis creep' occurs when a risk issue is ignored either because the company has learned to live with it over time, and therefore ignores the warning signs, or because it has failed to register developments in stakeholders' perceptions. Marks and Spencer was guilty of both when it failed to spot changes in consumer buying habits over a number of years. There was a growing perception among consumers and shareholders that the company was arrogant and failing to listen to its customers, leading to a gradual erosion of its market share and its reputation as a market leader. This inevitably affected share price and the company has spent the past year struggling to win back the confidence of its stakeholders.

Executives cite a variety of factors that prevent them from addressing issues which threaten reputation before a crisis occurs. Barriers to identifying 'crisis creep' issues include:

■ companies focusing on the short-term concerns of annual reporting and immediate risk issues, rather than advance planning;

■ a belief that size, location or the type of business will somehow protect them or that the product is immune from particular social pressures; and

■ anticipatory issues and crisis management are often seen as a luxury, or crisis is viewed as an inevitable cost of doing business. For instance, a survey in the early 1990s showed that prominent US businessmen believed a crisis in business was as inevitable as paying taxes and death.

The following points can help businesses to think about the three main areas in which 'crisis creep' can occur. In these areas, it is important to consider the links between stakeholder perception and corporate reputation. These are:

■ **The growing importance of business and service continuity.**
During the 1980s, it had become clear that customer care was a valuable asset, which often determined whether or not a company would weather a crisis. Today, customers expect a high level of continuous service and are increasingly intolerant of delays and lapses in customer care. Managers need to assess

factors that may disrupt smooth delivery of service. These may include competitive, technological, supply chain, regulatory, employee or broader social and economic factors of change.

■ **Profound changes in the relationship between business and society.**

In an era of the 'triple bottom line' – balancing commercial success, environmental quality and social justice – the stakes are becoming much higher for companies as they deal with the outside world. Adverse public opinion, amplified by a global electronic media and the workings of sophisticated single issue groups, can all too readily be channelled through litigation and in turn places pressure on government agencies to introduce tougher and costlier regulation.

Accountability and responsibility have become the watch-words of modern business. Industry is being forced to take over the traditional government mantle of 'providing and protecting'. There is a growing need to adopt an inclusive style of rela-tionship management with customers, shareholders, suppliers, public officials, consumer groups, employees and the media. It is vital to involve these different stakeholder groups in new developments and to provide them with information that can inform decision-making and maintain support.

The way in which businesses communicate external and internal developments – particularly around emotive issues such as health risks and legal responsibility – tends to determine their reputation.

■ **Corporate responsibility and liability.**

In the context of corporate responsibility, trends and legislative developments are placing new pressures on business to review operational and communication practices. For example, risk management and internal control have moved firmly onto the boardroom agenda. This is part of a growing trend.

The European Commission published a new communication in February 2000 clarifying that the precautionary principle should be applied when scientific evidence is insufficient, inconclusive or uncertain, and where there is a potentially dangerous effect on the environment, human, animal or plant health. This has major implications for the food industry, for example, and companies failing to apply this approach may find themselves subjected to individual director, as well as corporate, liability.

In the UK, the government has recently released a proposal for a new offence of corporate killing. This is part of a more general trend towards tougher penalties for individual company directors (including imprisonment), not simply for fatal accidents but also for damaging environmental and public health effects of commercial operations.

In addition, the remit of the Competition and Consumer Affairs portfolio at the Department of Trade and Industry has recently been extended to cover corporate social responsibility. This will cover issues such as ethical trading and promoting triple bottom line reporting. It will encourage active consumer and shareholder investment strategies that positively discriminate in favour of social responsibility policies and public disclosure by companies.

Stakeholder analysis: 'Outside-in' thinking

This complex and confusing climate requires organisations seeking to avoid 'crisis creep', and maximise commercial opportunity, to develop a flexible and intuitive approach to planning and decision-making. Successful companies are those which are outward-facing and which understand not only who their audiences are, but what they think and what they want. Yet there continue to be many examples of companies which have failed to put this thinking into practice.

'Outside-in' thinking – the ability to look at an organisation from the outside inwards – is essential. Organisations need to create and operate a risk radar screen with 360 degree vision that identifies, assesses and responds to the differing attitudes and behaviour of a host of stakeholder groups.

Fig. 3.3.2: The risk radar screen

Without an outside-in approach, organisations will fail to anticipate and respond to broader public perception. Public perception is generally shaped by complex emotional dynamics which organisations have, in the past, failed to understand. A failure to handle these dynamics can rapidly produce all the components of a crisis, with the resulting irreparable reputation and financial damage.

In more detail, 'outside-in thinking' may consist of risk planning and risk communication. The planning process requires senior management to:

- understand the potential risk and acknowledge it may exist;
- put in place early warning and monitoring systems (Risk Radar Screen);
- consider ways to improve operational and organisational processes;
- establish a clear process for communication;
- identify stakeholder groups and establish their information needs;
- utilise third party allies to build credibility;
- be responsive and communicate in ways that relate to the differing concerns of each stakeholder group;

- build investment, product and service benefits separately from the risks;
- monitor, evaluate and fine tune messages.

Effective risk communication can:

- reduce tension between business, shareholders and consumers;
- reduce barriers to market development and product acceptance;
- create a more conducive environment for investment;
- minimise the threat of increased regulation and litigation;
- establish long-term trust and credibility with stakeholders.

Contingency planning if a crisis occurs

Failure to have in place well-tried and tested contingency plans for every kind of emergency means that, when the unexpected does occur, a company can only assume a combative posture; it is, of necessity, put into a defensive frame of mind. Those who are alert to the possibility that any event, even a crisis, is an opportunity to gain allies, to enlist support and, possibly, even to encourage existing and new shareholders and customers, are well-prepared

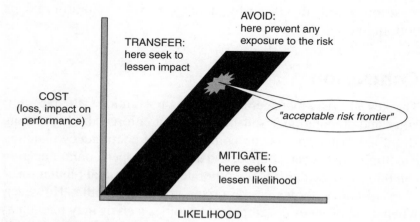

Fig. 3.3.3: Prioritising risk issues

to seize the initiative. A proactive posture can be established, which leads to a positive attitude rather than a siege mentality.

The media shapes stakeholder perceptions of whether or not a crisis was preventable and whether it is being handled well or badly by the company. It is often tempting for companies to dismiss media claims as 'hysteria': the reality may be that the crisis event is being handled extremely well from an operational standpoint, but if the organisation fails to tell its own story effectively, stakeholders will quickly perceive it to be mishandling the crisis. Successful crisis management is about being seen by stakeholders to take the appropriate action and heard to say the appropriate words.

In this context, successful crisis management boils down to managing stakeholder perceptions of:

■ how it happened;
■ the organisation's action to contain and control the crisis;
■ the organisation's expression of concern about the crisis;
■ how preventable the crisis was;
■ the organisation's commitment to change things to ensure it never happens again.

These perceptions can be summarised as the three 'C's: Concern, Control, Commitment. If an organisation in a crisis does not take these on board, it will suffer damage to its reputation and its bottom line.

Conclusion

The key to crisis management is crisis prevention, whether vigilance and preparation is self-motivated, or enforced by legislation. But if a disaster does occur, comprehensive contingency planning can minimise the catastrophe, and a policy of open communication can minimise the damage to corporate and individual reputation.

As history shows, some crises are unavoidable. However, whether an event or development becomes a crisis may be seen as largely in the hands of management. Moreover, management action plays a highly important role in either exacerbating or reducing the effects of a crisis if one does occur, through its handling of its key stakeholders. At the worst extreme, a nonchalant approach to a potential crisis can lead to total corporate collapse. At the best, companies that take an 'outside-in' approach and have their radar switched on, achieve much more than protecting their operations from failure. Such companies are far more sensitive to wider developments and perceptions, and gain valuable insights for forward planning and competitive, strategic management.

Michael Regester is a Founding Partner of Regester Larkin, the specialist risk and crisis communication consultancy. The consultancy specialises in providing planning, systems development and advice on how to exploit issues for commercial advantage and minimise risk impact. A Fellow of the Institute of Public Relations, Fellow of the International Public Relations Association, he has over twenty years' experience of international corporate communications and issues and crisis management. His publications include *Risk Issues and Crisis Management: A Casebook of Best Practice,* co-written with Judy Larkin.

Regester Larkin helps organisations to identify and manage the risk issues they face in order to safeguard competitive performance and reputation through tailored analysis and planning. Its services include a Risk Analysis Unit, dedicated to intensive research and surveillance of issues which could impact on an organisation's reputation and bottom line.

Launching products & services

Publicity is a vulgar word in PR, says Lesley Brend, Managing Director, The RED Consultancy. Product launches are about substance and no company should risk its long-term reputation for a short-term boost to sales. Microsoft and Johnson & Johnson provide two cases in point.

There is no such thing as 'just' a new product launch or 'just' a new service launch. Products and services are never islands – each one is part of a brand strategy and ultimately a master corporate strategy. Sure, that's the way it's always been – but nowadays there is far more corporate transparency and corporate accountability.

Consumers now invariably know who the product's parents are (they might even have shares in that parent) and they expect the 'child' to toe the line with the family code of conduct. In turn, the parent gets credit for good behaviour of the child and is held responsible for any of its wayward behaviour.

There was a time when product launches were all about 'publicity' – blanket exposure at all costs. Very occasionally you still get a 'black sheep' throwback to those days – a bad taste 'publicity stunt' is broadcast across the nation's media that leaves the parent company in corporate crisis mode fighting off irate pressure groups and public allegations of irresponsibility.

But whereas 'publicity' and product launches used to go hand in hand, publicity is now seen as a vulgar word in PR.

Instead, everything is about substance. The communications mantra is 'let's do a little, but do it well'.

No company wants to risk its long-term corporate reputation for the sake of short-term till receipts for a new product or service. On the contrary, they look for a product launch to enhance corporate reputation.

Take, for example, two recent winners of Public Relations Consultants Association (PRCA) Outstanding Professional Practice Awards. Yes, both generated high volumes of media coverage, but what singles them out as outstanding is their brand intelligence and their underlying corporate sensitivity.

Microsoft is a corporation with a capital C – one of the most famous companies in the world. As such every product launch sends out signals about the corporation and carries with it a corporate responsibility. A pathfinding company has to do pathfinding PR.

So when the e-commerce hullaballoo first started to break in the UK media in the early months of 1999, it was inappropriate for msn.co.uk, Microsoft's mainstream internet business, to dive in as just another face in the crowd.

While many other internet companies were fanning the flames of hype, what Microsoft decided to do was take a completely different stance – be human, be honest, be impartial.

That meant showing e-commerce as it really was by conducting the first real-life road test for UK online shopping. The PR initiative was coined 'four naked people alone with the Internet' and the question it set out to address was 'can man or woman live by the Internet alone?' Quite simply, what would happen if people were locked away for 100 hours with only a bathrobe, a PC and £500 on a credit card.

Four volunteers were hidden in a secret location and an expert in human computer interaction was recruited to evaluate the findings scientifically. The four appeared twice daily for global online interviews and were visible to the outside world through a webcam on their PC. In stark contrast to the hype that surrounded e-commerce at the time, these four 'ordinary' members of the British public gave their no-holds-barred views on UK e-commerce – the shortcomings as well as the benefits.

The exercise gripped the attention not just of the UK's media, but the world media, with the story running as far afield as South Africa, Australia, Chile, Brazil and the USA. What made it such a success was its depth. The findings were of genuine value to the Internet community – not just some quick hit, shallow media stunt.

Furthermore, it presented Microsoft corporately in a positive and appropriate light, as an honest, empathetic and innovative thought-leader that dared to be different, rather than one of the herd.

The launch of a new cellulite cream from RoC is another example of an award-winning new product launch which enhanced corporate reputation. A totally different market category to Microsoft, but again illustrative of how empirical objectivity and substance ultimately win the day in PR.

RoC is owned by Johnson & Johnson which has a 50-year-old heritage as a science-based, ethical, caring, trusted company. In the beauty market, cellulite creams were among the most controversial of products – and had been much criticised and lambasted.

Somehow, the trusted corporate reputation of Johnson & Johnson had to be reconciled with this 'untrusted' market category of cellulite creams. Corporate credibility was at stake.

In the world of 'wonder cures' that characterise the beauty market, what RoC did was adopt a no-hype, straight-talking strategy. The company decided the key to success was not over-promising in its claims.

At the same time, RoC took the unusual (and brave) step of pre-empting the cynics by hijacking the cynics' comments and embracing them in their own key messages. So the product message became 'This is NOT a miracle cure, you can't sit on the sofa eating chips and chocolate and think this cream will make your cellulite look better'.

Alongside this, RoC opted for an evidence-based factual and scientific approach where every claim could be supported empirically. As part of this, 50 women volunteers (including journalists) were enlisted to take part in independent clinical trials where they could see for themselves the efficacy of the product.

The product worked better on some than others, but in keeping with the 'honesty-first' strategy, all consumer trialists were invited to give their views, whatever those views were.

The product was launched to positive acclaim by the media and went on to become a bestseller at Boots.

The launch of the RoC cellulite product was fraught with risks – risks which could have fundamentally affected the ethical standing of the brand and corporation. But by throwing away the marketing textbook and focusing as much on what the cream didn't do (NOT a miracle cure) as on what it did do (improve the look of cellulite by toning the skin), it was a win/win result for both the product and corporate reputation.

In summary, great product launches shouldn't just 'sell and tell' the product, they should 'sell and tell' the corporation. Product launches aren't just about getting coverage in the media, they're about getting coverage in the media in an appropriate way that has a beneficial halo effect on the parent company. That means putting quality before quantity, substance before style.

Lesley Brend has been in PR since the early 80s and during this time has worked on campaigns for around 200 corporations and brands.

She is Managing Director and Joint Founder of The RED Consultancy, which was formed in 1994, and has gone on to win numerous awards for its work.

Reputations online

The rules for building reputations and brands online are not the same as offline says Mark Mellor, Director of Firefly, a digital economy specialist.

What do names like Amazon, Nike, Lastminute.com, Marks & Spencer, Click Mango, Boots, BP, AltaVista, CNN.com, Motley Fool, Red Herring and Reuters mean to you? Perhaps more apt is what did these names mean to you just 18 months ago and what do they mean now?

Hard-earned reputations are being made or broken in weeks as investors size up the bricks and mortar companies' abilities to mould themselves to the future, taking stock of young upstart dotcoms with great ideas but no track record and no profits on the horizon. Couple this with an interactive medium that can tear apart copyright law, replace customer loyalty with price-driven purchasing, and provide a live information feed to the world that is capable of bringing down governments and corporations, and the awesome power of the Internet is laid bare for all to see.

As businesses struggle to move fast enough to meet the demands of the digital economy, marketing teams have been forced to realign their traditional branding views to reflect the fact that, in the retail and financial services sector at least, savvy online consumer and investor power can count for everything. Go to a well-known retailer's website to buy now and if you are offered a list of store locations, what do you think? Go to the Companies House website and you will find that it is only 'open' for searches during weekday office hours, so you can certainly see whether their lights are switched on. Had you gone to OPEC's site for information during the oil price crisis, you would have found that it had been taken offline owing to protestor postings.

Although out-of-date by the time you read this, at the time of writing I had a surf through a few well-known names on the Internet. Boots' web shopping site was down, albeit with an apology. Natural health products site Click Mango had a very nice farewell 'going out of business' message from actress Joanna Lumley, and Mothercare took five minutes per page to load even with an ISDN line. Marks & Spencer was getting there with online commerce in its own style, but maybe too late to resurrect a ten year share price low and halt takeover rumours – for which numerous other links for information were available to me at a keystroke. I'd also just had a rather defamatory picture of a BP petrol station's new customer relations policy emailed to me, and my newsfeed told me that at least ten per cent of retail e-commerce was fraudulent.

Wow, what a dynamic world we live in and what a nightmare for reputation managers to cope with.

The world seems temporarily confused by the difference between notoriety and brand recognition. Many of the names we see advertised on the TV and radio this year will not be here next year. Indeed many of the longstanding names in the FTSE 100 will not be around either. The Internet is largely to blame, but is this such a bad thing when it makes companies more accountable, helps level prices for consumer goods and services across continents, and gives people access to their investments and bank accounts when they want it?

So is there such a thing as online brand values? I believe there is, and there are a number of fundamental differences between building an online brand and building an offline brand. A major difference is that the interactive experience of using the website becomes in many ways the product offered to the surfer. A website must not only look good and be easy to use, but there must be truly differentiated content and these days it must explore the interactive mechanisms available to attract 'stickiness' and provide a satisfying experience.

A website is not a place to re-publish brochureware, but a place to interact with and entertain business customers, consumers, partners, investors and employees. It is a place to inform and provide access, enabling a cost-effective communications transformation for businesses and public service organisations. The same rules apply for corporates' communications with the media: 85 per cent of FTSE 100 companies still have little more than posted press releases on their websites, rather than fully functional, interactive Internet press centres offering an array of sources, information and quality pictures.

Nobody can have escaped the dotcom phenomenon and there is no doubt that many in the advertising, PR, media, marketing (and recruitment!) worlds benefited from its explosive growth, but it is thankfully proving true that genuine dotcom brands are built on substance and not just image.

Analysing Amazon and Nike demonstrates the point. One achieves differentiation through breadth of offering, customer knowledge, service and ease of use, the other by sophisticated and aggressive imagery. Building an online brand is therefore about communicating substance and values, educating consumers or businesses about the benefits of using a particular website. Nike and Amazon must translate their brand culture into anything they do online. Traffic must be driven to these sites so that enough users experience the online brand and remember: websites grow mainly through word of mouth and PR can be a spur to spreading the word and a means of orchestrating it, ahead of the other marketing disciplines.

PR can also help establish the all important first mover advantage in the face of strong competition. Sometimes this means being the first to discuss a new Internet innovation, not necessarily being the first to deliver. Fsharp, the first Internet offshore bank and part of the Bank of Ireland, was the first to get into the media and discuss the potential of this market, even though the site was openly not going live for some time. The result is that Fsharpbank.com is branded as a real innovator and first mover in its sector. One need also only look at Amazon to see the value of this, and Lastminute.com operated on the same first-mover principle and got away with it shortly before investor sentiment soured towards the b2c Internet business model.

On the other hand, AltaVista gained huge awareness and first mover advantage launching the UK's first free Internet service, but later paid a bitter price when it became clear that it was not economically viable for any company to offer such a service under the UK telecoms regime. Age-old communications rules still apply and time will tell whether their reputation and brand values withstand this local episode, but they are a global brand.

A final, important difference between online and offline branding is speed of connection. Traditional branding may mean that a consumer sees an advert for a product, discusses it with a friend, buys a magazine for a review and finally goes into the shop to see the product. These are four lengthy moves between first contact and brand experience. Online connection can be much more effective and dynamic: the consumer sees a link, clicks on that link, and experiences the brand in one move – and can even buy the product as part of that move. PR is able to exploit this speed and dynamism by building links with like-minded websites and web communities that increase the likelihood of a consumer using that link. The world has turned topsy-turvy and in many sectors seemingly vehement competitors of the past have now turned unlikely partners-in-traffic behind the scenes.

Unfortunately, while the Internet provides opportunities, there are also pitfalls. With so many forums where people can discuss your brand, the potential for misinformation to spread and undermine that brand is high. Last year a chatroom rumour that information provider Dialog was in financial trouble saw seven per cent of its value wiped within hours. Such occurrences are now regular and the consequences even more dire. PR is the only marketing discipline that can react quickly and subtly enough to help prevent such problems with counter statements and a positive presence in such discussions. My only advice here is expect a disaster to happen and apply crisis management best practice – ie plan for it! Make sure you explore the range of web-monitoring tools available and ensure that you have a range of amalgamated online newsfeeds and search engines working for you. The Internet is a 24-hour a day global world, so prepare on that basis.

Online branding is a relatively new discipline, but in years to come it will be essential to business success. The traditional brands are potentially in a great position to exploit their names, but many are playing fiddles while the ship sinks. Investor relations will be transformed by the Internet and for consumer brands, loyalty among the growing online community at large will emerge, but probably where you least expect it.

Online Reputation Management Checklist

1. Think brand values and not just name awareness.
2. Evaluate your current online presence to ensure that it reflects your true values, engages the customer or user, and contains dynamic not static information.
3. Monitor the web, online media, newsgroups and chatgroups for your organisation's name or product names, or even your key executives' names if they are prominent personalities.
4. Create a comprehensive crisis management plan for handling online crises.
5. Remember to include online communications as a fundamental component of corporate reputation and brand building, and as a tool in the event of any crisis.

Mark Mellor has spent 18 years in marketing communications, the majority focused on PR consultancy for b2b and b2c technology and Internet clients. In recent years his Firefly clients have included Compaq, First Direct, IBM, ICL and Sony, the launches of BBC News Online and Lastminute.com, many Internet start-ups, business magazine *Red Herring*, and *Which?Online*.

Firefly is the UK's leading PR consultancy specialising exclusively in the digital economy. The company has been consistently voted No.1 in its sector in independent polls and has offices in London, Glasgow and Paris as well as a network of partners across Europe and USA.

Managing market sentiment

To build brand advantage in a market storm demands innovation and organisational flexibility within a clear set of values, argues Tim Kitchin of Ogilvy PR.

'Market sentiment' is such an innocuous phrase, but a queue of postponed IPOs stretching round the globe waits, in cash-strapped testament, to its importance. Yesterday's sure thing is today's long shot, and today's shining star is tomorrow's financial black hole – just ask clickmango.

The compelling question, for every (e)-business is, how to build and grow a valuable business in the midst of this chaos. How can businesses anticipate, interpret, respond to and manage such fast-shifting market opinion? The challenge is no longer to separate perception from reality, but to determine which perceptions will have most impact on a business and what, if anything, can be done about them.

We are all living in the midst of a market storm, and the excitement and fear are equally palpable. Hitherto sceptical bricks-and-mortar businesses are suddenly waking up and sending teams of their best people out into the rain, equipped only with a corporate T-shirt and a damp chequebook to buy up the spluttering dotcoms. In the midst of all the smash and grab, oblivious to the thunder and lightning, visionary people are still trying to build visionary businesses which can shape the future of markets. These successful corporate brands, whether born in the new or old economy, will be 'elastic' in the best sense.

The companies which successfully build elastic brands will be the 'built to last' companies of the 21st century.

Elastic brands will be those which can easily accommodate innovation and organisational flexibility within a clear set of brand values. 'Elastic' describes those organisations for which 'organisational agility' is not a mere management cliché, but is embedded in the culture, and is, in effect, a promise of the corporate brand. Easier perhaps, for a twenty-person dotcom in a Regus office block, but perfectly possible, even for an industrial-age icon like Ford, fast reinventing itself through some truly radical organisational and brand initiatives, but driven by a crystal-clear vision of a consumer-centric motor company.

Elastic brands allow companies to buck negative market sentiment, or even when they do suffer, allow them to return faster to their former stature (and valuation-level) when sentiment shifts back. IBM's return to being one of the world's most valuable brands, after its mid-90s slump to 286th in a *Fortune* survey, is a perfect example of long-term brand elasticity. Its recovery is obviously testament to leadership and extraordinary management, but also to a brand which acted as a rallying-point to the workforce who would be required to turn around one of the world's largest and most complex organisations. Brand-loyal employees ultimately provide the tension and responsiveness in a corporate brand.

Truly elastic brands should also elicit an apparently disproportionate response when they make positive announcements. This doesn't just mean that they will trade off a high (and sustainable) p/e ratio, but rather it is a broad measure of market confidence in its widest sense, reflecting the basis of long-term trust from partners, suppliers and investors alike. A more stable, long-term investor base, attentive and constructive stakeholder relationships, and educated, open analyst relationships, are both causes and effects of brand elasticity.

Finally, at the heart of brand elasticity lies arguably the most important corporate asset of all, brand-loyal customers. The arguments in favour of customer retention and growth are well-rehearsed, but the long-term impact on the corporate brand is perhaps less evident. While short-term perceptions of a company may waver, the earned loyalty of its core customers can act as a significant brake on any long-term reputation-slippage.

Elasticity results from a complex combination of positive perceptions: leadership, strong management, uniqueness, vision, transparency and accountability. But these good, old-fashioned corporate virtues are not merely a source of long-term differentiation – they are a survival kit for the New Economy.

Despite apparent market corrections, the storm is actually just beginning. As business models we have only just begun to understand spawn increasingly complex hybrids, the pendulum of market opinion is likely to oscillate ever faster. Alone and half-blind, businesses will continue to rely upon analysts, media and self-appointed 'gurus', who will wield greater and greater influence. As any management consultant will tell you, 'in the kingdom of the paranoid, the therapist is king'.

The enduring winners will be the elastic brands, which remain single-minded in their vision; but responsive to changes in the market, who understand what's negotiable and what isn't and stick by those principles, come what may. They will be those who stay close to their customers, but lead and exceed their expectations. Finally, long-term success will come to those who have deep and mutually-trusting relationships with all their stakeholders.

Elastic brands make great corporate catapults.

Ogilvy Public Relations Worldwide
Global

Ogilvy Public Relations Worldwide was recognised as the 2000 Agency of the Year by *PRWeek US* and is the second fastest growing firm in the top 10 (*PRWeek UK*).

Headquartered in New York, Ogilvy PR partners with clients throughout the world from over 50 offices in 46 markets across Europe, Asia, Africa and the United States. There is also a strong network of local and global affiliate relationships as part of WPP Group, the world's largest marketing communications company.

Ogilvy PR has grown rapidly and this has led to some of the world's leading brands trusting their public relations programmes to Ogilvy PR. The company also continues to attract staff members of the very highest calibre right across the globe.

Around the world, Ogilvy PR has specialty practices in Health and Medical, Marketing, Corporate and Public Affairs. The Technology Practice now operates under the Alexander Ogilvy PR brand.

Evaluating messages

Communications research has wider applications than tracking media profiles, says Sandra Macleod at Echo Research. It reveals a wealth of information on brands, share prices and customer satisfaction.

Confidence capital, sometimes called reputational capital, has taken its place alongside an organisation's other assets – physical assets, intellectual assets and market capital.

As a result, organisations are eager to measure their 'confidence capital' both direct and in the media, and how it impacts on media-consuming stakeholders.

That's why evaluating messages the media sends to reading, listening, viewing and Internet-accessing publics, and how those publics pick them up, has become such a respected strategic research tool. The need for media analysis alone has, in the last 10 years, spawned an industry worth at least £15 million in Europe alone. This figure is likely to rise as communications functions are urged to go for the industry standard of ten per cent research and evaluation out of total budgets.

The business case for media evaluation usually flows from the ability to analyse communications impact: 'how well will/did/is the campaign work(ing)?'. But considered as a significant contact with your brands, the media carry extra clout. The brand contact becomes doubly vital when corroborated by other indices. For there are demonstrable impacts on customer satisfaction levels from the quality of coverage. Share prices are driven by media sentiment. Voting preferences ebb and flow with media debate, most feverishly before elections. Integration of these data creates a tremendously powerful source of brand intelligence.

So a pile of press cuttings, tapes and web downloads can be transformed into a chiaroscuro of the key issues, the messages playing for or against you, the journalists and titles who are running stories even-handedly or grinding pet axes.

Media analysis can track imbalance: over lunch with a utility chairman, a journalist on a national that prides itself on balance was shown media analysis evidence that the paper had favoured the utility's critics, which was fed back to the news and features desks.

Proactive communications – positive newsmaking rather than waiting for someone else's story about you to break – can be logged to measure how you triggered good coverage or intervened to repair damage. All this highlights PR's linchpin role.

Coming through in the analysis, too, are third parties – customers, opinion-formers, analysts, regulators, politicians – whose support as allies needs nurturing, or whose discontent as critics demands damage limitation. The 'reach and frequency' data of each paper or programme reveals volumes about who's been exposed to the ebb and flow of messages, by gender, income, political persuasion, lifestyle, buying power and mindset.

Another research dividend is intelligence from tracking competitors' activity: the messages they put into the marketplace, how their share of voice fares and how well they come through.

Media analysis has a radar function too. It identifies emerging indices of what's round the corner next, fed in through a journalist's specialist knowledge, or via influential players quoted in the story. To the informed reader it can offer marketing opportunities, and, based on analysis of overseas media, insight into geographical regions where it would cost far more to gather intelligence on the ground.

Armed with such information, corporate communicators and PR teams can adapt and shape their communications efforts, in a bid to better manage how they are reported. Again there are industry standards recommending a cycle of excellence for marketing communications, running from pre-action audits to campaign feedback to performance assessment, to recalibrating and resetting targets.

Besides these vital nuts-and-bolts uses, communications research is a real performance yardstick. Business performance, once assessed only by the hard indices of the profit and loss account and productivity, is now quantified through 'softer' measures like management style, client relationships, innovation, environmental record, the standing of the chief executive. Reputation, as the umbrella concept for these 'soft' issues, has acquired value on the corporate balance sheet. It has been estimated as worth between 8 and 15 per cent of the share price, or two years' turnover.

Reputation is not a monolithic attribute. Like a diamond it has facets, varying by stakeholder. The key 'virtues' appreciated by each group are the sparkle on each facet. Each virtue therefore needs to be identified and communicated and perceptions measured. For example, for customers the communications target might be reliability of product/service; the relevant communications measurement/key performance target may therefore be to raise by 40 per cent the presence in selected trade media of the message 'the company's products are high-quality'; or to move two points ahead of the main competitor on the brand descriptor 'trustworthy'. Similarly, to be perceived as credible to investors, the targets could be to raise favourability of endorsements by city analysts in selected 'Premier League' financial media from 45 to 52 per cent; or to increase by ten per cent support on an investors' panel of the message 'the company has growth prospects'. By the same token, a measure for the target that one should be thought of as responsible by the community could be to sustain positive coverage of community relations initiatives at six million local opportunities-to-see (circulation totals). Or again, a measure of increasing success in being regarded as trustworthy by employees could be to increase from less than 50 per cent to over 60 per cent the numbers of team members who say in employee surveys that the company gives them a sense of empowerment.

In terms of business intelligence and management information, then, communications research, including media analysis, has a tactical role as a tool for communications teams, and strategically as radar and performance indicators for the board.

Sandra Macleod is Chief Executive of global specialist in reputational audit, Echo Research. With a background in communications and management consultancy, Sandra has lectured and advised clients across five continents.

A leader in its field, Echo is unique in integrating traditional and innovative research and evaluation tools which allow its 100+ world-class clients to establish their own guidelines for future success. Whether global or local, focused on internal or external communications, or interpreting the link between communication achievements and organisational objectives, out clients are helped to:

- demonstrate communications effectiveness;
- evaluate image and reputation across target audiences and key stakeholders;
- assess competitors' perceived strengths and weaknesses.

Echo works for more than one-quarter of the FTSE 100 companies, governments and NGOs.

The logistics of
name changes

A change in name signalled more than a new identity for Sodexho in the UK. It was a conscious effort to forge a new reputation. Claire Meredith explains.

Background

On 21 February 2000, Gardner Merchant, the UK's best known catering company, adopted the name of its French parent company, Sodexho, a brand virtually unknown in the UK.

Rationale for the name change

The rationale behind this decision was twofold. First, market research indicated that the Gardner Merchant name was known primarily for contract catering. This perception restricted the company's expansion into the support services sector. Second,

Sodexho, as the world's leading catering and support services company, was a powerful global brand and it became clear that Gardner Merchant could benefit from this international presence.

Strategy

The strategy was to use the change of brand identity as a platform for accelerating the repositioning of the business from a company known primarily for catering to a total support service provider. The decision was taken to change the name on a specific date – literally overnight – rather than to use dual branding for an initial period. This required a fully integrated internal and external communications campaign that would take place over a three-year period.

Strategic objectives

- Make brand awareness of Sodexho as strong in the UK and Ireland as the Gardner Merchant brand over three years. At the time of the name change, Gardner Merchant had 66 per cent spontaneous awareness and 98 per cent prompted awareness.
- Establish Sodexho's reputation in the UK as a leading provider of catering and support services, building on its experience as market leader in the catering sector.
- Differentiate Sodexho, through its support service offer, from its competitors.
- Retain the heritage and values of the Gardner Merchant brand.
- Strengthen existing client relationships and open up new business leads.
- Motivate 53,000 employees in 3,500 locations to live the new corporate vision, values and goals.

Tactics

Once the Board approved the name change, a fully integrated communications strategy was developed covering three distinct phases:

- bridging phase, 12 months prior to launch;
- announcement phase, January to end March 2000;
- reinforcement phase, March 2000 – March 2002.

Market research:

Research was conducted with clients, prospects and employees on the Gardner Merchant and Sodexho reputations as well as their reaction to the name change. This established a platform for the subsequent communications programme. On this basis, a series of initial advertisements was developed, tested and adapted as appropriate.

Initial preparation:

In order to prepare the marketplace for the name change, a series of roadshows entitled 'Vision 21' were hosted in the key cities of London, Birmingham, Manchester and Glasgow. Employees, clients, prospects and the media attended the events where the company showcased its full service offering and outlined the company strategy and vision. These events aimed to position the company as innovative, forward-thinking and in touch with changing customer demands. In fully interactive sessions the audience took part in discussions and research through voting pads. Again this data was collated and bench-marked for the ensuing communications strategy.

Employee communication:

Due to their close interaction with clients and prospects, employees were a key target audience. It was critical that the workforce not only understood the benefits of the name change but also that they communicated this to clients and prospects through their everyday work. Senior management, including the Chief Executive, became part of the implementation team at the earliest stage and this was then expanded to employees at all levels through a series of focus groups and regional workshops. Staff received brochures, briefing packs and videos as part of the communications rollout.

Client communications:

Clients were briefed locally by account management teams on the name change and its corporate objectives. They also received a letter from David Ford, Chief Executive, and a corporate brochure outlining the new corporate vision and material on Sodexho. Prospective clients received a specially designed direct mail programme including corporate CD Roms.

Media:

The Sodexho brand was introduced gradually to the media, during the bridging phase, by referring to the Sodexho parent company in all media releases and information. Media hooks included the Sodexho Research Institute into the Quality of Daily Life that is dedicated to examining customer needs and demands and helped raised awareness of the Sodexho name in the media. At the time of the name change, research was carried out to look into increasing stress levels in the workplace. The research highlighted the value of support services in this environment and, hence, the corporate repositioning.

Advertising and sponsorship:

Advertising consisted of national, regional and trade press and local radio. During the week of the name change Sodexho sponsored the AXA ATP tennis tour, and co-sponsored the *Daily Telegraph* Business Team Golf Championships and the Senior Tour Golf Match Play in Portugal.

Logistics:

The company had to:

- send 53,000 letters to employees;
- organise 11 focus groups;
- book venues for workshops and run workshops for managers in 22 divisions to explain the campaign;
- produce videos and brochures;
- arrange for new re-branded stationery, signage and uniforms;
- schedule announcements for press and radio and internal magazines;
- contact national, regional and trade media;
- train telesales teams, sales secretaries, co-ordinators and consultants;
- issue new instructions to managers who commission printed materials;
- organise 19 roadshows for 4,500 managers and one supplier roadshow;
- organise research to include evaluation of Sodexho brand awareness;
- review all existing materials of sales teams such as display boards, written material and CD Roms;
- design and mail brochure and letter to clients;
- change IT support systems;
- register new company names;
- plan for company credit cards, bank cheques etc to be re-issued.

Outcome and evaluation

Employees:

Market research showed a high level of understanding of the main messages communicating the rationale behind the name change and the corporate repositioning. Employee morale was high, with

96 per cent showing positive attitudes towards the new organisation and strong confidence in the future success of Sodexho. This endorsement was critical in communicating the key messages to the outside world.

Existing and prospective clients:

Market research showed that there was high recognition of the Sodexho name and that the brand maintained the positive benefits of the Gardner Merchant name. Significantly, not one contract was lost as a result of the name change and new business has been at an all time high since. Overall with both clients and prospects, 40 per cent of the market recall the advertising and 60 per cent, when prompted, recall the name change.

■ Research undertaken in October 2000 has shown that spontaneous awareness of the Sodexho name has risen from 3 per cent – before the name change – to 29 per cent and prompted awareness from 15 per cent to 55 per cent.

Media:

A high level of coverage was achieved, communicating the key messages around the name change and corporate repositioning. This included articles in the major trades, national and regional newspapers, including the front page of the *Financial Times*, 15 radio interviews and four television slots.

Costs:

The campaign will cost a total of £4 million over the three years.

Sodexho Alliance is the largest catering and support services provider in the world, employing over 280,000 in 70 countries. Gardner Merchant became a member of Sodexho Alliance in 1995 and adopted the Sodexho name for its operations in February 2000.

In the UK and Ireland, Sodexho provides catering and a range of support services to clients in the business and industry, education, healthcare, leisure and defence sectors. The company is dedicated to providing service at a local level through its 55,000 staff at over 3,500 client locations.

4

Directory of
PRCA Members

The Public Relations Consultants Association

A S Biss & Co

Ms Adele Biss
100 Rochester Row
London
SW1P 1JP
T: 020 7828 3030
F: 020 7828 5505
E: tellmemore@asbiss.com

Abel Hadden & Company Ltd

Mr Abel Hadden
15 Berkeley Street
London
W1X 5AE
T: 020 7629 8771
F: 020 7629 8772
E: abel@ahadden.com

AD Communications Ltd

Mr Richard Allen
The Old Post House
81 The High Street
Esher, Surrey
KY10 9QA
T: 01372 464470
F: 01372 468626
E: richard@adcommunications.co.uk

Attenborough Associates Ltd

Mr Nick Attenborough
Waverley House
7–12 Noel Street
London
W1F 8NN
T: 020 7734 4455
F: 020 734 4507
E: nicka@attenborough.net

Audax Communications

Ms Rosie Featherstone
5 Castle Quay
Castle Boulevard
Nottingham
NG7 1FW
T: 0115 941 7887
F: 0115 9240991
E: pr@audax.co.uk

AUGUST.ONE Communications

Mr Tariq Kwaja
Network House
Wood Lane
London
W12 7SL
T: 020 8434 5555
F: 020 8434 5755
E: tariq.khwaja@augustone.com

Barclay Stratton Ltd

Ms Jenny Thomas
River House
33 Point Pleasant
London
SW18 1NN
T: 020 8877 8600
F: 020 8877 8620
E: jenny.thomas@barclaystratton.co.uk

Barkers Public Relations

Ms Dianne Page
Kennedy Tower, Snow Hill
Birmingham
B4 6JB
T: 0121 236 9501
F: 0121 233 4156
E: d.page@barkers-birmingham.co.uk

Barrett Dixon Bell

Ms Suzanne Bell
25 Hale Road
Altrincham
Cheshire
WA14 2EY
T: 0161 925 4700
F: 0161 925 4701
E: henry@bdb.co.uk

Biss Lancaster plc

Ms Isobel Greenwood
69 Monmouth Street
London
WC2H 9DG
T: 020 7497 3001
F: 020 7497 8915
E: isabel@bisslancaster.com

BMB Reputation Managers

Ms Stella Hitner
Bute Mills, Mill Yard
Guildford Street
Luton
LU1 2NH
T: 01582 406003
F: 01582 406113
E: stella@reputationmanagers.co.uk

Brodeur Worldwide

Mr Guy Douglas
New Tithe Court
23 Datchet Road
Slough
SL3 7PT
T: 01753 790700
F: 01753 790701
E: gdouglas@uk.brodeur.com

BSMG Worldwide

Mr David Brain
110 St Martin's Lane
London
WC2N 4DY
T: 020 7841 5458
F: 020 7841 5777
E: dbrain@bsmg.com

Buffalo Communications Ltd

Ms Kerry Hallard
44 Wardour Street
London
W1X 6L
T: 020 7385 0777
F: 020 7385 8662
E: info@buffalo.co.uk

Bulletin International UK Ltd

Ms Lucy Tilbury
5–9 Hardwick Street
London
EC1R 4RG
T: 020 7278 6070
F: 020 7278 6349
E: lucy.tilbury@uk.bulletin.com

Burson-Marsteller

Ms Fiona Couper
24–28 Bloomsbury Way
London
WC1A 2PX
T: 020 7831 6262
F: 020 7430 1033
E: fiona_couper@uk.bm.com

Carrot Communications Ltd

Mr Richard Houghton
28 Bruton Street
London
SW6 6AW
T: 020 7927 8330
F: 020 7927 8374
E: richard.houghton@carrotcomms.co.uk

Chambers Cox PR Ltd

Ms Rose Gibson
7/8 Rathbone Place
London
W1P 1DE
T: 020 7631 5414
F: 020 7580 7719
E: rose@ccpr.co.uk

Citigate PLPR

Mr Alan Burnside
157–159 High Street
Holywood
Belfast
BT18 9HU
T: 028 9039 5500
F: 028 9039 5600
E: alan.burnside@citigateni.co.uk

Citigate Public Affairs

Mr Simon Nayyar
26 Grosvenor Gardens
London
SW1W 0GT
T: 020 7838 4800
F: 020 7838 4843
E: simon.nayyar@citigatepa.co.uk

Citigate SMARTS

Ms Flora Martin
231–233 St Vincent Street
Glasgow
G2 5QY
T: 0141 400 1770
F: 0141 400 1771
E: angela.mckay@citigatesmarts.co.uk

Citigate Westminster Ltd

Mr Adrian Roxan
26 Grosvenor Gardens
London
SW1W 0GT
T: 020 7838 4800
F: 020 7838 4801
E: info@citigatew.co.uk

Clareville Consultancy

Mr John Starr
315–317 New Kings Road
London
SW6 4RF
T: 020 7736 4022
F: 020 7736 3504
E: john@clareville.co.uk

CLEAR

Mr John Underwood
143–145 Farringdon Road
London
EC1R 3AB
T: 020 7833 5655
F: 020 7833 5855
E: lesley@clearco.co.uk

Cohn & Wolfe Ltd

Mr Jonathan Edwards
30 Orange Street
London
WC2H 7LZ
T: 020 7331 5300
F: 020 7331 9083/4/5/6/8
E: jonathan_edwards@ukcohnwolfe.com

Collette Hill Associates Ltd

Ms Colette Hill
Polygon House
18–20 Bromell's Road
London
SW4 0BG
T: 020 7622 8252
F: 020 7622 8253
E: colette@chapr.co.uk

Communication Group Scotland

Ms Claire Meikle
2 York Place
Edinburgh
Scotland
EH1 3EP
T: 0131 557 6767
F: 0131 556 1133
E: cmeikle@tcg-scot.co.uk

Communique PR

Mr Paul Carroll
Waterside
2 Canal Street
Manchester
M1 3HE
T: 0161 228 6677
F: 0161 228 7391
E: paul.carroll@communique-pr.co.uk

Companycare Comms

Mr Ian McCann
154 Castle Hill
Reading
Berks
RG1 7RP
T: 0118 939 5900
F: 0118 959 9595
E: info@companycare.com

Condor Public Relations Ltd

Ms Tina Hancock
299 Oxford Street
London
W1R 1LA
T: 020 7499 7324
F: 020 7495 1106
E: tina@condorpr.co.uk

Consolidated Communications Management Ltd

Mr Alastair Gornall
1–5 Poland Street
London
W1V 3DG
T: 020 7287 2087
F: 020 7734 0772
E: alastair@consol.co.uk

Countrywide Porter Novelli Ltd

Mr Neil Backwith
South Bar House
Banbury
OX16 9AD
T: 01295 224400
F: 01295 224444
E: neil.backwith@cpn.co.uk

Countrywide Porter Novelli Scotland

Ms Angela Casey
Hanover House
45 Hanover Street
Edinburgh
EH2 2PJ
T: 0131 470 3400
F: 0131 470 3444
E: angela.casey@cpns.co.uk

Darwall Smith Associates Ltd

Ms Gill Garside
113–117 Farringdon Road
London
EC1R 3HJ
T: 020 7833 5833
F: 020 7833 5900
E: gill@dsapr.co.uk

Edelman Public Relations Worldwide

Ms Tari Hibbitt
Haymarket House
28/29 Haymarket
London
SW1Y 4SP
T: 020 7344 1200
F: 020 7344 1222
E: Tari.Hibbitt@edelman.com

Edson Evers & Associates

Mr Keith Webb
New Garden Street
Stafford
ST17 4AG
T: 01785 255146
F: 01785 211518
E: pr@edsonevers.co.uk

Elizabeth Hindmarch

Ms Elizabeth Hindmarch
16 Park Street
Windsor
SL4 1LU
T: 01753 842017
F: 01753 856661
E: info@ehpr.co.uk

EuroPR Group

Mr Richard Price
22–24 Worple Road
London
SW19 4DD
T: 020 8879 3033
F: 020 8947 9042
E: rprice@europrgroup.co.uk

Firefly Communications Ltd

Ms Kieran Moore
25/4 The Coda Centre
189 Munster Road
London
SW6 6AW
T: 020 7386 1400
F: 020 7385 4768
E: kieran.moore@firefly.co.uk

Flagship Group

Ms Diana Soltmann
140 Great Portland Street
London
W1N 5TA
T: 020 7299 1500
F: 020 7299 1550
E: diana.soltmann@flagshipgroup.co.uk

Fleishman-Hillard

Mr Paul Blackburn
25 Wellington Street
London
WC2E 7DA
T: 020 7306 9000
F: 020 7497 0096
E: blackbup@fleishman.com

Focus PR Ltd

Ms Hilary Meacham
7–9 Swallow Street
London
W1B 4DX
T: 020 7432 9432
F: 020 7432 9433
E: hilary@focuspr.co.uk

Garnett Keeler Public Relations

Mr David Bellis
60/63 Victoria Road
Surbiton
Surrey
KT6 4NQ
T: 020 8399 1184
F: 020 8390 7465
E: pr@garnett-keeler.com

GCI Financial

Mr Rupert Ashe
80 Cannon Street
London
EC4N 6BJ
T: 020 7398 0800
F: 020 7398 0888
E: rashe@gcifinancial.com

GCI Healthcare

Mr Alan Archer
New Bridge Street House
30–34 New Bridge Street
London
EC4V 6BJ
T: 020 7072 4100
F: 020 7072 4012
E: aarcher@gciuk.com

GCI London

Ms Sue Ryan
New Bridge Street House
30–34 New Bridge Street
London
EC4V 6BJ
T: 020 7072 4000
F: 020 7072 4010
E: sryan@gciuk.com

GMX Public Affairs

Mr David Abraham
Vigilant House
120 Wilton Road
London
SW1V 1JZ
T: 020 7808 7976
F: 020 7808 7977
E: info@gmxpa.com

Golin/Harris International

Ms Sue Farr
The Courtyard
30 New Oxford Street
London
WC1A 1AP
T: 020 7898 3333
F: 020 7898 3334
E: sfarr@golinharris.com

Golin/Harris Ludgate

Mr Robin Hepburn
111 Charterhouse Street
London
EC1M 6AW
T: 020 7324 8888
F: 020 7324 8880
E: rhepburn@golinharris.com

Golley Slater Public Relations

Ms Althea Taylor-Salmon
St George's House
3 St George's Place
Twickenham
TW1 3NE
T: 020 8744 2630
F: 020 8891 6994
E: ataylor-salmon@golleyslater.co.uk

Grandfield Ltd

Mr Nick Boakes
69 Wilson Street
London
EC2A 2BB
T: 020 7417 4170
F: 020 7417 9180
E: nick.boakes@grandfield.com

Grant Butler Coomber Group

Ms Neil Vose
Westminster House
Kew Road
Richmond
TW9 2ND
T: 020 8322 1922
F: 020 8322 1923
E: neilv@gbc.co.uk

Grayling Group

Mr Nigel Kennedy
4 Bedford Square
London
WC1B 3RA
T: 020 7255 1100
F: 020 7631 0602
E: pr@graylinggroup.co.uk

Green Light Communications

Mr Nigel Bartlett-Twivey
Airport House
Purley Way
Croydon
CR0 0XZ
T: 020 8633 8600
F: 020 8633 8601
E: greenlight@greenlightuk.com

Hallmark PR

Dr Tom Watson
Canister House
27 Jewry Street
Winchester
SO23 8RY
T: 01962 863850
F: 01962 841820
E: twatson@hallmarkpr.co.uk

Harrison Cowley Ltd

Ms Denise Mullen
Dragon Court
27 Macklin Street
London
WC2B 5LX
T: 020 7404 6777
F: 020 7404 6888
E: denisem@harrisoncowley.com

Haslimann Taylor

Ms Bronwen Eames
11 Wrens Court
Victoria Road
Sutton Coldfield
B72 1SY
T: 0121 355 3446
F: 0121 355 3393
E: info@haslimanntaylor.com

Herald Communications

Ms Sarka Klofacova
7th Floor, Artillery House
11–19 Artillery Row
London
SW1P 1RT
T: 020 7340 6300
F: 020 7340 6400
E: sklofacova@heraldcommunications.com

Hill & Knowlton

Ms Marie Louise Windeler
35 Red Lion Square
London
WC1R 4SG
T: 020 7413 3000
F: 020 7413 3111
E: info@hillandknowlton.com

Icas Public Relations

Mr Carl Courtney
19 Garrick Street
London
WC2E 9BB
T: 020 7632 2400
F: 020 7240 2520
E: carl@icas.co.uk

JBP Associates Ltd

Ms Linda Taylor
The White House
6 Whiteladies Road
Bristol
BS8 1PD
T: 0117 907 3400
F: 0117 907 3417
E: linda@jbp.co.uk

Kable PR

Ms Anna Hooper
49/50 Great Marlborough Street
London
W1V 1DB
T: 020 7734 0063
F: 020 7734 0067
E: ahooper@kablepr.co.uk

Kaizo

Mr Crispin Manners
66–68 Margaret Street
London
W1N 7FL
T: 020 7580 8852
F: 020 7580 5035
E: paul.smith@kaizo.net

Kavanagh Communications

Ms Anne Kavanagh
The Old Dairy
Highway Farm
Cobham
KT11 3JZ
T: 01932 866010
F: 01932 868799
E: info@annekavanghpr.co.uk

Ketchum

Mr Jon Higgins
35–41 Folgate Street
London
WC2E 7HA
T: 020 7611 3500
F: 020 7611 3501
E: anna.burns@ketchumcomms.com

Key Communications Ltd

Mr David Watson
First Floor, Kings Court
2–16 Goodge Street
London
W1P 1FF
T: 020 7580 0222
F: 020 7580 0333
E: davidw@keycommunications.co.uk

Kinross & Render Ltd

Ms Sarah Render
192–198 Vauxhall Bridge Road
London
SW1V 1DX
T: 020 7592 3100
F: 020 7931 9640
E: sara@kinross-and-render.co.uk

Lansons Communications

Mr Tony Langham
42 St John Street
London
EC1M 4DL
T: 020 7490 8828
F: 020 7490 5460
E: tonyl@lansons.com

Lawson Dodd Ltd

Ms Joanna Dodd
12 Great Portland Street
London
W1N 5AB
T: 020 7580 1945
F: 020 7580 1985
E: directors@lawsondodd.co.uk

LawsonClarke Ltd

Mr Jeremy Clarke
4 Dollar Street
Cirencester
G17 2AJ
T: 01285 658844
F: 01285 650080
E: clarke@lawsonclarke.co.uk

Leader Communications Ltd

Mr James Holden
The Stone House
123 High Street
Henley-in-Arden
B95 5AU
T: 01564 796200
F: 01564 795490
E: jbh@leader.co.uk

Leedex Euro RSCG

Ms Sarah Muirhead
69 Monmouth Street
London
WC2H 9DG
T: 020 7497 0110
F: 020 7836 4913
E: sarah.muirhead@leedex.com

Lexis Public Relations Ltd

Ms Claire Smith
8 Bolsover Street
London
W1P 7HG
T: 020 7908 6488
F: 020 7908 6490
E: csmith@lexispr.co.uk

Maclaurin

Mr Brian MacLaurin
Berghem Mews
Blythe Road
London
W14 0HN
T: 020 7371 3333
F: 020 7471 6898
E: ceo@maclaurin.com

Manning Selvage & Lee Ltd

Ms Jackie Elliot
123 Buckingham Palace Road
London
SW1W 9SH
T: 020 7878 3000
F: 020 7878 3030
E: results@mslpr.co.uk

Marbles

Ms Sue Beard
48 Hart Street
Henley-on-Thames
Oxfordshire
RG9 2AV
T: 01491 411789
F: 01491 413313
E: sbeard@marbles.co.uk

Mason Williams Ltd

Mr John Williams
7–11 Lexington Street
London
W1F 9AF
T: 020 7534 6080
F: 020 7534 6081
E: john@mason-william.com

McCann Erickson Public Relations

Ms Claire Oliver
King Edwards Court
Sutton Coldfield
West Midlands
B93 9LH
T: 0121 321 2444
F: 0121 321 2442
E: claire_oliver@europe.mccann.com

Midnight Communications

Ms Caraline Brown
Tower Point
North Road
Brighton
BN1 1YR
T: 01273 666200
F: 01273 666201
E: enquiries@midnight.co.uk

Miller Shandwick Technologies

Ms Cathy Pittham
35 King Street
Covent Garden
London
WC2E 8JD
T: 020 7240 8666
F: 020 7240 8668
E: cpittham@miller.shandwick.com

Mistral

Mr Mike Evans
Cassington
Oxford
OX8 1EB
T: 01865 883308
F: 01865 881969
E: mike.evans@mistral-pr.co.uk

Montpellier Marketing Comms

Mr Guy Woodcock
Glendale House
Montpellier Terrace
Cheltenham
GL50 1UX
T: 01242 262977
F: 01242 236141
E: guy@montpelliergroup.com

Munro & Forster Communications Ltd

Ms Alison Munro
89 Albert Embankment
London
SE1 7TP
T: 020 7815 3900
F: 020 7815 3999
E: alison_munro@munroforster.com

Nelson Bostock Communications Ltd

Mr Paul Hildrew
Compass House
22 Redan Place
London
W2 4SA
T: 020 7229 4400
F: 020 7792 7401
E: paul@nelsonbostock.com

Nexus Choat Public Relations

Ms Veronique Briant
Bury House
126–128 Cromwell Road
London
SW7 4ET
T: 020 7373 4537
F: 020 7373 3926
E: veroniqueb@nexuschoat.co.uk

Oakes Bacot

Mr Eugene Bacot
58 Queen Anne Street
London
W1M 9LA
T: 020 7224 0994
F: 020 7224 5952
E: eugene@oakesbacot.co.uk

Ogilvy Public Relations Worldwide

Ms Donna Zurcher
Porters Place
11–33 St John Street
London
E14 4QB
T: 020 7309 1032
F: 020 7309 1001
E: donna.zurcher@uk.ogilvypr.com

Partnership Plus

Mr John Haschak
112–114 Thorpe Road
Norwich
NR1 1RX
T: 01603 611031
F: 01603 630206
E: pr@partnership-plus.co.uk

Paskett PR

Mr Graham Paskett
50–51 Friar Gate
Derby
DE1 1DF
T: 01332 372196
F: 01332 291096
E: info@paskett.co.uk

Peretti Communications Ltd

Ms Francoise Peretti
58 Jermyn Street
London
SW1Y 6LX
T: 020 7915 4777
F: 020 7915 4778
E: francoise.p@peretti.com

Peter Sawell & Partners Ltd

Mr Peter Sawell
1 Nelson Road
London
SE10 9JB
T: 020 8858 5771
F: 020 8305 1726
E: psp_pr@compuserve.com

Phipps Public Relations

Mr Nick Hindle
33 Long Acre
London
WC2E 9LA
T: 020 7759 7400
F: 020 7759 7402
E: nick.hindle@phippspr.co.uk

Portfolio Communications Ltd

Mr Mark Westaby
Russell Chambers
The Piazza
London
WC2E 8AA
T: 020 7240 6959
F: 020 7240 4849
E: mark.westaby@portfoliocomms.com

PPR

Ms Christine Mortimer
Devonshire Court
Devonshire Avenue
Leeds
LS8 1AY
T: 0113 226 2210
F: 0113 268 1436
E: christine.mortimer@ppr-pr.co.uk

PPS Group Ltd

Mr Nick Keable
69 Grosvenor Street
London
W1X 9DB
T: 020 7629 7377
F: 020 7629 7514
E: nick.keable@ppsgroup.co.uk

PR21

Ms Beverley Kaye
67–69 Whitfield Street
London
W1P 5RL
T: 020 7436 4060
F: 020 7255 2131
E: karen.sells@pr21.com

Ptarmigan

Mr Gordon Forbes
Airedale House
423 Kirkstall Road
Leeds
LS4 3EZ
T: 0113 242 1155
F: 0113 242 1588
E: gordon@ptarmiganpr.co.uk

Raitt Orr & Associates Ltd

Mr Patrick Orr
36 Buckingham Palace Road
London
SW1W 0RE
T: 020 7828 5961
F: 020 7630 9750
E: raittorr@compuserve.com

Red Rooster Beauty and Consumer PR Ltd

Ms Tanya Lake
The Media Centre
131–151 Great Titchfield Street
London
W1P 7FR
T: 020 7665 8400
F: 020 7665 8401
E: misst@rrpr.com

Regester Larkin Ltd

Mr Michael Regester
16 Doughty Street
London
WC1N 2PL
T: 020 7831 3839
F: 020 7831 3632
E: mregester@regesterlarkin.co.uk

Republic

Ms Jane Howard
Dudley House
36–38 Southampton Street
London
WC2E 7HE
T: 020 7379 5000
F: 020 7379 5122
E: jane@republicpr.com

Roger Staton Associates Ltd

Mr Roger Staton
Old Trinity Church
Trinity Road
Marlow
SL7 3AN
T: 01628 487222
F: 01628 487223
E: mail@rsagroup.com

Rowland Communications

Mr Richard Moss
83–89 Whitfield Street
London
W1A 1AQ
T: 020 7462 7766
F: 020 7462 7967
E: richard.moss@rowlandcomms.co.uk

Shine Communications

Ms Rachel Bell
101 Goswell Road
London
EC1V 7ER
T: 020 7553 3333
F: 020 7553 3330
E: brilliance@shinecom.com

Shire Hall Communications

Ms Sarah Harwood
3 Olaf Street
London
W11 4BE
T: 020 7313 6300
F: 020 7313 6301
E: sarah.harwood@shirehall.co.uk

Smithard Associates

Mr Barry Smithard
452 Oakleigh Road North
London
N20 0RZ
T: 020 8368 9666
F: 020 8368 3824
E: smithard@smithard.co.uk

Staniforth Communications

Mr Phil Staniforth
2 Whites Grounds
London
SE1 3LA
T: 020 7940 7999
F: 020 7940 7998
E: urgent@staniforth.co.uk

Starfish Communications

Mr Julien Speed
Oxford House
76 Oxford Street
London
W1N 0HP
T: 020 7323 2121
F: 020 7323 0234
E: speed@star-fish.net

Storm Communications

Mr Derek Lowe
19 London End
Beaconsfield
HP9 2HN
T: 01494 670444
F: 01494 670333
E: derek@stormcom.co.uk

Target Consultancy

Ms Sheena Brand
Victoria House
St James Square
Cheltenham
GL50 3PR
T: 01242 633100
F: 01242 584417
E: sheena_brand@targetgroup.co.uk

Text 100

Ms Katie King
Power Road Studios
114a Power Road
London
W4 5PY
T: 020 8996 4117
F: 020 8996 1217
E: katieki@text100.co.uk

The Communication Group plc

Mr Peter Hamilton
19 Buckingham Gate
London
SW1E 6LB
T: 020 7630 1411
F: 020 7931 8010
E: phamilton@tcg-pr.co.uk

The Dialogue Agency

Ms Cherry Haigh
Regal House
70 London Road
Twickenham
TW1 3QS
T: 020 8607 0340
F: 020 8607 0341
E: enquiry@dialogueagency.com

The Impact Agency

Ms Linda Batt-Rawden
3 Bloomsbury Place
London
WC1A 2QL
T: 020 7580 1770
F: 020 7580 7200
E: linda@impactagency.co.uk

The Quentin Bell Organisation plc

Mr Trevor Morris
22 Endell Street
London
WC2H 9AD
T: 020 7379 0304
F: 020 7379 5483
E: trevorm@qbo.com

The RED Consultancy

Mr David Fuller
77 Wimpole Street
London
W1M 7DD
T: 020 7465 7700
F: 020 7486 5260
E: red@redconsultancy.com

The WhiteOakes Consultancy Ltd

Ms Sarah Shave
26–27 Downing Street
Farnham
GU9 7PD
T: 01252 727313
F: 01252 727314
E: sarahs@whiteoaks.co.uk

TMA Public Relations

Mr Tony Meehan
9 Woodside Crescent
Glasgow
G3 7UL
T: 0141 333 1551
F: 0141 333 1661
E: tmeehan@tmac.co.uk

TTA Public Relations

Ms Tricia Topping
9 Sutton Court Road
Sutton
SM1 4SZ
T: 020 8770 6720
F: 020 8643 5393
E: headoffice@tta-pr.co.uk

VLP

Mr John Levick
2nd Floor, India House
45 Curlew Street
London
SE1 2ND
T: 020 7403 7500
F: 020 7403 6714
E: info@vlp.co.uk

Warman & Bannister

Mr Simon McKay
Meadowcroft
Church Street
Cambridge
CB4 1EL
T: 01223 314545
F: 01223 324611
E: SimonM@warban.com

Warman Group

Mr Robert Warman
8 The Wharf
Bridge Street
Birmingham
B1 2JS
T: 0121 605 1111
F: 0121 605 0111
E: enquiries@warmangroup.com

Weber Europe

Ms Cathy Pittham
2 Endell Street
London
WC2H 9BL
T: 020 7240 6189
F: 020 7240 6195
E: zarden@webergroup.co.uk

Weber Shandwick Worldwide

Mr Lutz Meyer
Aldermary House
10–15 Queen Street
London
EC4N 1TX
T: 020 7329 0096
F: 020 7329 6009
E: ebowen-davies@webershandwick.com

Westbury Communications

Ms Sue Harris
3 Imperial Studios
3–11 Imperial Road
London
WC1N 2PL
T: 020 7404 5575
F: 020 7831 8733
E: sue.harris@westburycom.co.uk

Willoughby Public Relations

Ms Julia Willoughby
36–37 Cox Street
St. Paul's Square
Birmingham
B3 1RD
T: 0121 233 1130
F: 0121 233 1181
E: juliaw@willoughby-pr.co.uk

5

Directory of ICCO Members

The International Communications Consultancy Organisation

The International Communications Consultancy Organisation (ICCO) was formed in 1986. Its main objectives are:

- to share information on all relevant aspects of Association activities and consultancy management practice;
- to work towards harmonisation of standards;
- to increase awareness of the value of professional PR consultancy practice.

More information is available on ICCO's website at **www.iccopr.com**

ICCO Board of Management

David Drobis (USA)
President
Ketchum
711 Third Avenue
18th Floor
New York, NY 10017
USA
T: +1 646 935 3901
F: +1 646 935 3924
E: david.drobis@ketchum.com

Jean-Léopold Schuybroek (Belgium)
Vice President
Interel Marien Group
Avenue Tervueren 402
B-1150 Brussels
Belgium
T: +32 2 761 66 10
F: +32 2 777 05 07
E: jls@intermar.be

Jean-Pierre Beaudoin (France)
Past President
Information et Entreprise
32 Rue De Trevise
75009 Paris
France
T: +33 1 5603 12 12
F: +33 1 5603 13 13
E: jean-pierre_beaudoin@I_et_e.fr

Guido Bellodi (Italy)
Past President
Chiappe Bellodi Srl
Via Carducci 16
20123 Milan
Italy
T: +39 02 809 946
F: +39 02 877 058
E: guido.bellodi@bellodi.inet.it

Peter Hehir (UK)
Past President
Countrywide Porter Novelli International
South Bar House
South Bar
Banbury
OX16 9AD
United Kingdom
T: +44 1295 224400
F: +44 1295 271757
E: peter.hehir@cpn.co.uk

Lex Schoevers (Netherlands)
Past President
Hill and Knowlton Nederland BV
PO Box 87360
1080 JJ Amsterdam
The Netherlands
T: +31 20 404 4707
F: +31 20 644 9736
E: lschoevers@hillandknowlton.com

Chris McDowall
Secretary General
ICCO
Willow House
Willow Place
London SW1 1JH
United Kingdom
T: +44 207 233 6026
F: +44 207 828 4797
E: chris@prca.org.uk

Christian Koenig (Switzerland)
Treasurer
Farner PR
Oberdorfstrasse 28
8001 Zurich
Switzerland
T: +41 1 266 6767
F: +41 1 266 6700
E: Koenig@farner.ch

Ole Christian Apeland (Norway)
Member
Norske Informasjon Radgivere
Skjolden 1
1322 Hovik
Norway
T: +47 67 56 67 56
F: +47 67 56 67 51
E: ole@apeland.com

Evzen Cekota (Czech Republic)
Member
Mozaic
Na Porici 12
115 30 Prague 1
Czech Republic
T: +42 02 2487 5320
F: +42 02 2487 5322
E: cekota@mozaic.cz

Alvaro Esteves (Portugal)
Member
Média Alta – Imagem & Comunicação, Lda
R.D. Francisco Manuel de Melo, 1–3 Esq
1070–085 Lisbon
Portugal
T: +351 21 386 9116
F: +351 21 387 9499
E: media.alta.com@mail.telepac.pt

Peter Forssman (Sweden)
Member
Gullers PR
PO Box 7004
S-103 86 Stockholm
Sweden
T: +46 8 679 0957
F: +46 8 611 0780
E: peter.forssman@gullers.se

Tari Hibbitt (UK)
Member
Edelman PR Worldwide
Haymarket House
28/29 Haymarket
London SW1Y 4SP
United Kingdom
T: +44 207 344 1266
F: +44 207 344 1295
E: thibbitt@edelman.com

Salim Kadibesegil (Turkey)
Member
ORSA
Mektep Sokak No. 30
80620 Levent
Istanbul
Turkey
T: +90 212 283 5599
F: +90 212 283 6057
E: skadibesegil@prciturkey.com

Jarkko Kuusinen (Finland)
Member
Carta Communications Ltd
Aleksanterinkatu 46A
00100 Helsinki
Finland
T: +35 89 615 4600
F: +35 89 615 4664
E: jarkko.kuusinen@carta.fi

Carlos Lareau (Spain)
Member
Burson-Marsteller
Avda. De Burgos, 21 – 7 PI
Complejo TRIADA Torre C
28036 Madrid
Spain
T: +34 91 384 6700
F: +34 91 766 5995
E: Carlos_Lareau@es.bm.com

Maria Lazarimou (Greece)
Member
The PR Team
51 Vas. Sofias Str
106 71 Athens
Greece
T: +301 729 3580–2
F: +301 729 3583
E: maria_lazarimou@yr.com

Jacques Marceau (France)
Member
Aromates SA
169 rue d'Aguesseau
92100 Boulogne-Bilancourt
France
T: +33 1 46 99 10 80
F: +33 1 46 04 70 98
E: jmarceau@aromates.fr

Adriana Mavellia (Italy)
Member
Mavellia Relazioni Pubbliche Srl
Corso Venezia 16
20121 Milan MI
Italy
T: +39 02 77 33 61
F: +39 02 77 33 6360
E: a.mavellia@mavellia.it

Vibeke M Mestanas (Denmark)
Member
Mestanas & Partners
Strandgade 36
DK-1407 Copenhagen K
Denmark
T: +45 32 96 82 82
F: +45 32 96 82 85
E: vibeke@mestanas.dk

Sergei Mikhailov (Russia)
Member
Mikhailov & Partners PR
24/35, B.5 Krzhizhanovskogo St.
Moscow 117259
Russia
T: +70 95 956 3972
F: +70 95 956 3973
E: sergem@mikh-partn.ru

Bozidar Novak (Slovenia)
Member
SPEM
Gregorciva 39
2000 Maribor
Slovenia
T: +38 6 6222 2787
F: +38 6 6222 3209
E: bozidar.novak@spem-group.com

Renate Skoff (Austria)
Member
The Skills Group
Weyringergasse 28A
A-1040 Vienna
Austria
T: +431 505 2625
F: +431 505 9422
E: skoff@theskillsgroup.com

Hannemie Stitz (Germany)
Member
Public Relations Partners Gesellschaft
Bleichstraβe 5
(PO Box 1310, 61468 Kronberg)
61476 Kronberg
Germany
T: +49 6173 92 6700
F: +49 6173 92 6767
E: stitz@prpkronberg.com

Michaela Benedigova (Slovakia)
Observer
Interel
Kladnianska 12
821 05 Bratislava
Slovakia
T: +421 7 4342 2978
F: +421 7 4333 0003
E: benedigova@interel.sk

Ludmyla Datsenko (Ukraine)
Observer
Light Promotion
Room 8,9; Floor 9
49/51 Zhylianska Str
Kyiv 252114
Ukraine
T: +38 044 22 585
F: +38 044 22 06 044
E: ldatsenko@scholzandfriends.kiev.ua

Julia Lajos (Hungary)
Observer
Headline
H-1136 Budapest
Pannonia U. 15
Hungary
T: +361 339 8372
F: +361 339 8245
E: headline@kerszov.hu

Prema Sagar (India)
Observer
Genesis PR
30.AR Complex, RK Puram
New Dehli 110066
India
T: +91 (11) 611 8454
F: +91 (11) 688 1733
E: psagar@genesispr.com

6

Appendix

List of Contributors

Biss Lancaster Euro RSCG

69, Monmouth Street
London WC2H 9JW
T: 0207 497 3001
F: 0207 497 8915
Contact:Graham Lancaster, Chairman
E: graham.lancaster@bisslancaster.com
W: www.bisslancaster.com

BSMG Worldwide

640, Fifth Avenue
New York, NY – 10019
T: +212 445 8000
F: +212 445 8001
Contact: Harris Diamond, President and CEO
E: hdiamond@bsmg.com
W: www.bsmg.com

Citigate Public Affairs

26 Grosvenor Gardens
London SW1W 0GT
T: 020 7838 4853
F: 020 7838 4840
Contact: Simon Nayyar, Executive Director
E: Simon.nayyar@citigatepa.co.uk

CPRF

11, Penn Plaza
5th Floor
New York
New York 10001
T: +215 493 5579
Contact: Jack Bergen, President
E: jdbergen@prfirms,org

Echo Research

Friary House
Station Road
Godalming
Surrey GU7 1EX
T: 01483 413 600
Contact: Sandra Macleod, Chief Executive
E: sandraM@echoResearch.com
W: www.echoResearch.com

Edelman

Haymarket House
28–29 Haymarket
London SW1Y 4SP
T: 020 7344 1200
Contact: Tari Hibbitt, Chief Executive
W: www.edelman.co.uk

Equity.i.Plc

30 John Street
Bloomsbury
London WC1N 2AT
T: 020 7405 7777
F: 020 7405 7773
Contact: Brian Basham, Deputy Chairman

Firefly Communications

T: 020 7386 1426
Contact: Mark Mellor, Director
E: mark.mellor@firefly.co.uk
W: www.firefly.co.uk

Fishburn Hedges

77, Kingsway
London WC2B 6ST
T: 020 7839 4321
F: 020 7242 4202
Contact: John Williams, Chairman
E: john@williams-network.com
W: www.fishburn-hedges.com

GCI UK

1, Chelsea Manor Gardens
London SW3 5PN
T: 020 7351 2400
F: 020 7352 6244
Contact: Adrian Wheeler, CEO
E: pr@gciuk.com
W: www.gciuk.com

Hallmark Public Relations

Canister House
27 Jewry Street
Winchester SO23 8RY
T: 01962 863 850
F: 01962 841 820
Contact: Dr Tom Watson, Managing Director

Hill & Knowlton

35, Red Lion Square
London WC1R 4SG
Contact: Andrew Laurence, Joint Chief Executive

The Intelligence Factory

T: +1 212 210 3004
Contact: Ira Matathia, CEO
E: Ira_Matathia@nyc.yr.com
W: www.intelligencefactory.com

Ketchum

711 Third Avenue
New York
New York 10017
T: 646 935 4144
Contact: David Drobis, Chairman

Kinross & Render

192–198 Vauxhall Bridge Road
London SW1V 1DX
T: 020 7592 3100
F: 020 7931 9640
Contact: Sara Render, Chief Executive

Ogilvy PR

Porters Place
11–33 St John Street
London EC1M 4GU
T: 020 7309 1032
F: 020 7309 1001
Contact: Donna Zurcher

The Public Relations Consultants Association

Willow House
Willow Place
London SW1P 1JH
T: 020 7233 6026
F: 020 7828 4797
E: info@prca.org.uk
W: www.prca.org.uk
Contact: Wendy Richmond, Assistant Director

The RED Consultancy

77, Wimpole Street
London W1M 7DD
T: 00 44 7465700
Contact: Lesley Brend, Managing Director
E: red@redconsultancy.com

Regester Larkin

16, Doughty Street
London WC1N 2PL
T: 020 7831 3839
F: 020 7831 3632
Contact: Michael Regester, Founding Partner

Weber Shandwick Worldwide

Aldermary House
15 Queen Street
London EC4N 1TX
T: 020 7950 2000
F: 020 7950 2001–03–23
Contact: Chris Genasi, Chief Executive Corporate

Smythe Dorward Lambert

55, Drury Lane
London WC2B 5SQ
T: 020 7379 9099
F: 020 7379 7156
Contact: John Smythe, Chairman